THE SOMERSET and DORSET JOINT RAILWAY

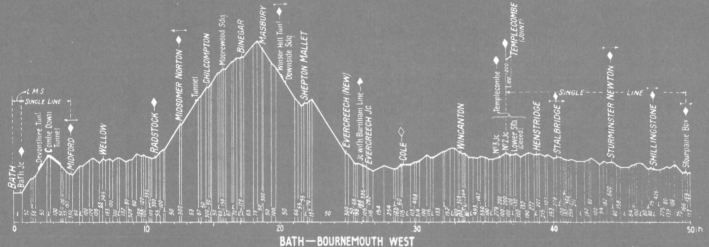

BATH—BOURNEMOUTH WEST

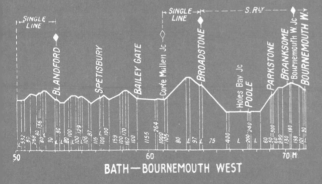

BATH—BOURNEMOUTH WEST

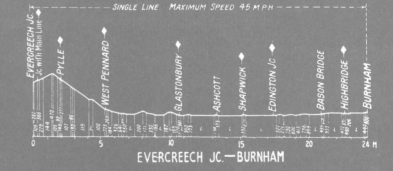

EVERCREECH JC.—BURNHAM

gradient profiles by permission of the Railway Magazine.

The Somerset & Dorset

An English Cross-Country railway.

by

IVO PETERS B.E.M.

Oxford Publishing Co · Oxford

SBN 0 902888 33 1

Printed by B. H. Blackwell in the City of Oxford and bound by Wigmore Bindery, Poole, Dorset.

The gradient profiles are reproduced by kind permission of the "Railway Magazine".

The train times quoted throughout this book are from the Working Time Table. (SO) after a train time indicates that the train ran only on Saturdays during the summer service.

To all my Somerset & Dorset friends, whose kindness and co-operation always made photography on the S & D such a very happy affair.

Photo Reproduction by Oxford Litho Plates Limited

Published by:—
Oxford Publishing Co.
5 Lewis Close
Risinghurst
Headington
Oxford

INTRODUCTION

Few cross-country lines can have been so full of character and charm as the Somerset and Dorset which ran from Bath to Bournemouth. To be strictly accurate, the main line of the Somerset and Dorset Joint Railway — to give the line its full title — only ran from Bath Junction to Broadstone, for at Bath Junction the Midland Railway was joined for the final half mile run into Bath, whilst at Broadstone, connection was made with the London & South Western Railway, and Somerset & Dorset trains used the South Western line for the remaining 8 miles of the journey to Bournemouth.

The Somerset & Dorset Railway was born in 1862, the result of an amalgamation between the Somerset Central Railway and the Dorset Central Railway. By 1863 the main line of the new Company ran from Burnham-on-Sea in Somerset to Wimborne in Dorset. From Wimborne, Somerset & Dorset trains could use the London & South Western line to reach the Hamworthy Station at Poole on the South Coast.

It was anticipated that substantial traffic would be attracted to this cross-country link between the Bristol Channel and the English Channel. When this failed to materialise, the Company, which was already in dire financial straits, decided to gamble everything on one last desperate bid for increased traffic, and built an extension from Evercreech Junction to Bath to join up with the Midland Railway. This new line, in addition to giving a rail outlet to several coal mines and stone quarries in North Somerset, provided a through route between the industrial Midlands and the North of England, and the South Coast and must, surely, produce a substantial increase in traffic. It did, but sadly too late to save the Somerset & Dorset, for the building of the Bath extension had brought complete financial exhaustion to the Company. There was nothing left but to offer the line to one of the large and wealthy Railway Companies and in 1875 the Somerset & Dorset was leased jointly to the Midland Railway and the London & South Western Railway.

The two types of S & D class 7F, 2-8-0 standing side by side on Bath shed in February, 1950. no. 53801 was one of the original batch of six built specially for the Somerset & Dorset by the Midland Railway at Derby in 1914. They had boilers of 4′9⅛″ diameter and right hand drive. No. 13807 — still with her L.M.S. number — was one of a further batch of five built in 1925 by Robert Stephenson & Co. They had larger boilers of 5′3″ diameter and left hand drive.

For the next 47 years the Midland and the London & South Western ran the Somerset & Dorset Joint Railway with success. The new route to Bath carried rapidly increasing traffic and became the main line; the original Somerset Central main line between Evercreech Junction and Burnham-on-Sea became "The Branch". Improvements to the Railway were steadily carried out. Many miles of single-line were doubled and in 1885 a new line was built from Corfe Mullen to join the London & South Western Railway at Broadstone, so shortening the route to Bournemouth and cutting out the tedious reversal process previously necessary for all Somerset & Dorset trains at Wimborne.

Then in 1923 the many separate Railway Companies in Great Britain lost their individuality when they were amalgamated to form just four large groups. The Midland was swallowed up in the London Midland & Scottish Railway, and the London & South Western became part of the Southern Railway — but the Somerset & Dorset Joint Railway continued almost unchanged, somehow even managing to keep the beautiful dark blue livery for its passenger engines for the next 7 years.

Even after the railways of Great Britain had been nationalised in 1948, the line continued to be referred to officially as "The Somerset & Dorset Line" and some Somerset & Dorset customs, such as the unique S & D headlamp code — one lamp under the chimney and one over the left-hand buffer for passenger trains, and one lamp under the chimney and one over the right-hand buffer for goods trains — were retained right up to the end of the line in 1966.

The Staff of the Somerset & Dorset was like one large family, nearly everyone seeming to know everyone else, and they all had immense pride in their Line. In the early 1960s, the fire buckets at Midford Station still had S. & D.J.R. painted on them, and on commenting about this to Percy Savage, one of the Midford signalmen, with 46 years railway service, his reply was "Yes, nice to see the buckets still correctly lettered isn't it?"

Much of the character and charm of the Somerset & Dorset lay in the immense physical difficulties which confronted the Railway and the manner in which they were overcome. When the Bath extension was built, the Mendip Hills offered a tremendous challenge, for rising to almost 1000 feet they lay directly in the path planned for the line. To tunnel through this barrier was quite out of the question, for as already mentioned, money for the project was very short. There was therefore only one alternative and that was for the Railway to climb over the Mendips. This necessitated long and very severe gradients which in turn made the Somerset & Dorset one of the most difficult lines to work in the whole of the Country.

The fire buckets at Midford in 1962 — still "correctly lettered".

As southbound trains left Ràdstock, they were confronted immediately with 7½ miles of almost unbroken climbing, much of it at 1 in 50, before reaching Masbury Summit, 811 feet above sea level. The test for trains travelling north was even more severe, for the bank started right from the platform end at Evercreech Junction and over the next 5 miles up to Shepton Mallet the climbing was almost entirely at 1 in 50.

After a brief respite through Shepton Mallet, there followed a further 3-mile uphill battle culminating in an extremely difficult section of 1 in 50 where the line had to forge its way upwards through a narrow, twisting, rock cutting before finally reaching the summit.

But it was not only long and severe gradients that had to be contended with on the Somerset & Dorset, for to add to the operating difficulties, no less than 23 miles of the main line were single track. This occurred between Bath Junction and Midford, Templecombe and Blandford Forum, and Corfe Mullen and Broadstone, and in times of peak traffic these sections could produce major problems, with trains blocked back for several sections at both ends, waiting their turn for use of the one line.

The pictures in this book have been chosen in an endeavour to bring out some of the atmosphere, character and charm of the Somerset & Dorset. The scenery throughout the whole length of the line was always interesting and much of it very beautiful; perhaps some of the best was just south of Bath where the line ran through the Midford and Wellow Valleys in a series of sweeping reverse curves following closely one after the other.

Several of the photographs have been specially selected to show the Somerset & Dorset 7F 2-8-0 freight locomotives which rendered such magnificent service for 50 years, from their introduction in 1914, right up to the day when the last one, No. 53807, was withdrawn on the 5th September, 1964. These engines were designed specially for the Somerset & Dorset by Sir Henry Fowler, and six were built in the Midland Railway Works at Derby in 1914. So successful were they that a further five were constructed in 1925 by Robert Stephenson & Company of Darlington. This second series was very similar to the original batch. However, they had left instead of right hand drive and were fitted with larger boilers of 5′3″ diameter as compared with 4′9⅛″ of the Derby built engines. In due course, as the 1925 series required reboilering, some began to be fitted with boilers of 4′9⅛″ diameter, and by the autumn of 1955 all eleven engines of the class had the smaller boiler and were therefore very similar in outward appearance.

The Somerset & Dorset 7F 2-8-0s were freight locomotives, but from 1950 onwards they often had to be pressed into service on summer Saturdays for hauling passenger trains during times of intense traffic.

An event of considerable importance for the Somerset & Dorset was the trial over the line on the 29th March, 1960 of a British Railways Standard Class 9F 2-10-0. The weather on the day of the test run was appalling with high winds and driving rain, but the locomotive, No. 92204, set to haul 350 tons unassisted, was most ably handled by driver Bill Rawles and came through the test with flying colours.

As a result, four 9F 2-10-0s were transferred to Bath Motive Power Depot for working the heavy weekend passenger trains which ran over the line during the summer service.

The arrival of the 9Fs on the Somerset & Dorset eased the locomotive situation considerably since, being permitted to take 410 tons unassisted, they obviated the necessity for much double heading which previously had been *sine qua non* for any train of over eight coaches unless hauled by a Somerset & Dorset 7F 2-8-0, which were permitted to take ten.

The pictures in this book have been arranged in "journey order", taking one down the line from Bath to Bournemouth, and concluding with a run up the Branch from Evercreech Junction to Burnham-on-Sea. A map of the line and a gradient profile have also been included for additional interest in following the journey down to Bournemouth and along the Branch.

For many years I had the good fortune to be granted a permit by the British Transport Commission giving me access to the Somerset & Dorset line for the purpose of taking photographs. For this privilege I am deeply grateful, since without it I could not have taken many of the pictures which appear in this book.

BATH,
SOMERSET

IVO PETERS 1973

1 Ex Midland 0-4-4T. no.58072 basks in the evening sunshine whilst collecting her two coaches from the middle road, to form the 6.5 p.m. local to Binegar.

BATH, GREEN PARK, STATION.

When the Somerset & Dorset was extended to Bath, arrangements were made with the Midland Railway to join their line on the western outskirts of the City at a point to become known as Bath Junction. From Bath Junction, the Midland Railway allowed Somerset & Dorset trains to run over their line for the last half mile into Bath and also to use the Midland Terminus.

The Midland Station, which in latter years became known as Bath, Green Park, was a pleasant small terminus with two platforms. Actually four lines ran into the station, but the two middle ones were used for "running round" and storage respectively. An attractive arched roof spanned all four tracks and covered the eastern end of the terminus.

2 Afternoon departure. Class 2P 4-4-0 no.40697 sets off at 4.26 p.m. with the 3.30 p.m. Bristol to Bournemouth, whilst in the other platform, 2-6-2T, no.41240 prepares to draw out the stock of the 12.55 p.m. up local from Bournemouth which had arrived at 4.23 p.m. Standing in the middle road, waiting for one of the platforms to become vacant, is ex-Midland 2P 4-4-0 no.40509 with the 4.37 p.m. down local for Templecombe.

3

Evening arrival. Ex L. & S.W.R. Class T9, 4-4-0 no.30706 standing in Bath station after bringing in the 3.35 p.m. from Bournemouth. The appearance of a T9 on the Somerset & Dorset was a rare occurrence. On this occasion, Bournemouth Central motive power depot had turned out no.30706 at short notice to replace a B.R. Standard class 4 which had failed.

4 The Somerset & Dorset Shed which was largely constructed of wood, had four roads and could accommodate up to 18 locomotives. The brick built coaling stage replaced an earlier wooden structure which was dismantled in 1954. The roof of the Midland shed can just be seen behind the coaling stage, and in the middle distance is Bath, Green Park, station. Standing outside the S & D shed on 14th July, 1962, are two Stanier class 5, 4-6-0s nos.44775 and 44888, and two 9F, 2-10-0s nos.92210 and 92001. On the right of the picture are three more Stanier "Black Fives", standing outside the old Midland shed.

BATH MOTIVE POWER DEPOT

5

The Somerset & Dorset shed was on a lower level than the surrounding tracks, and engines were faced with a short but sharp climb to reach the main line. A visitor from the North, 4-6-0 no.46100 *Royal Scot*, found some difficulty in keeping her feet as she came off shed to work a northbound express from Bath.

6 The Midland shed was situated on the same level as the main line. Although much smaller than the S & D shed, it was of far more solid construction, being built of stone throughout. The entrance to the Midland shed was via a 60′ turntable. On shed in this picture, taken on 6th September, 1964, are ex G.W.R. Pannier tank no.8745, B.R. class 5, no.73092 and S & D class 7F, 2-8-0 no.53807. Behind the 7F, in store, are four Stanier locomotives, two 2-8-0s and two 4-6-0s.

7 Three Somerset & Dorset stalwarts — 2P, 4-4-0 no.40700, 7F, 2-8-0 no.53807 and 4F, 0-6-0 no.44557. A constantly changing variety of motive power was used on the Somerset & Dorset, but each of these three classes of locomotive gave over 40 years service to the line.

8 Class 2P, 4-4-0 no.40601 being watered and coaled, whilst sister engine no.40698 waits her turn.

BATH MOTIVE POWER DEPOT

9

The turning of a class 9F 2-10-0 on Bath's 60′ turntable, called for care and precision, for the wheelbase of these locomotives was 55′11″ and their overall length 66′2″. If the engine was positioned just a little too far forward, then, as the turning proceeded, the leading buffers would foul wagons standing on the coal stage road. The positioning of a Southern Pacific had to be even more precise, for these engines had a wheelbase of 57′6″ and an overall length of 67′4¾″. With their 140 ton locomotive in position, the crew of no.92224 found it required quite an effort to coax the turntable into action.

10 Three class 2P, 4-4-0s and a Stanier "Black Five" lined up in the sunshine outside the S & D shed. Nos.568 and 40697 are ex L.M.S. engines with 6′9″ driving wheels. No.40505, one of the older ex Midland engines, had driving wheels of 7′0½″. This picture, taken in 1950, shows the old wooden coaling stage on the right.

11 A picture taken inside the S & D shed, shortly after the railways of Britain had been nationalised, and showing the timber trussed roof. The locomotive on the left — still with her L.M.S. number — is a 7F, 2-8-0, no.13807, one of the large boilered 1925 series. Behind her stands a 4F, 0-6-0. On the right is another 7F, no.53810 (her new B.R. number), also one of the 1925 series, but rebuilt with one of the smaller boilers of 4′9⅛″ diameter.

12

Ex L.M.S. class 2P, 4-4-0 no.40700 and B.R. class 4, 2-6-0 no.76028 have taken over the 9.15 a.m. (SO) ex-Birmingham and are setting off with the train for Bournemouth. The start is fairly gentle because, as they have left from the northern platform of the terminus, they will shortly have to traverse the cross-over taking them onto the down line.

SETTING OFF FROM BATH

13

9F, 2-10-0 no.92224 passes the bracket signal by Bath station signal box as she gathers speed with the 1.10 p.m. Bath to Bournemouth on 14th September, 1963. For many years a Midland signal, similar in lay-out but of wooden construction and with lower quadrant arms, stood in this position until replaced in June 1956 by this more modern structure made of steel.

14 On setting off from Bath station, S & D trains had a half mile run on the level over the Midland line before swinging south at Bath Junction onto the Somerset & Dorset, and the start of the climb out of Bath. As class 2P, no.40634 and Stanier "Black Five" no.44839 approach Bath Junction with the down "Pines Express", both engines are working hard so as to get up as much speed as possible for the coming attack on the 1 in 50 bank out of Bath. The mechanical tablet catching arm on the class 5 has been extended, ready to pick up the single-line token at Bath Junction.

15

At the beginning of March 1954, two Southern 2-6-0s, a class U and a U1, each spent a week hauling a series of test trains between Bournemouth and Bath to evaluate their suitability for use over the Somerset & Dorset. The results did not come up to expectations and, after the end of the fortnight test period, neither the U, nor the U1, appeared again regularly over the Somerset & Dorset. S.R. U class 2-6-0 no.31621 is seen running into Bath on 1st March, 1954, with the 11.40 a.m. from Bournemouth, specially made up to eight coaches for the test.

BATH JUNCTION

The Somerset & Dorset's own track commenced at Bath Junction. After leaving the Midland, the line — now single — started to climb immediately at 1 in 50, turning through a long, sweeping curve towards the south east.

17 The up "Pines Express" coming in over Bath Junction, hauled by class 7F, 2-8-0, no.53810 and 9F, 2-10-0, no.92001 — the most powerful locomotive combination ever seen on the Somerset & Dorset. This unique pairing of engines came about due to the failure of the booked assisting engine, a 2P, 4-4-0, the 7F being commandeered at short notice as a stand-in.

16 In April, 1955, Bath motive Power Depot was allocated two additional B.R. class 5, 4-6-0s. The locomotives came from the Southern Region, and no.73073 arrived on 23rd April, piloting class 2P, 4-4-0 no.40564 on the up "Pines Express" — seen here drifting in over Bath Junction. Although Great Western — and later, Western Region — preference when working double-headed trains was for the more powerful engine to be in front, the Somerset & Dorset did not follow this practice. If assistance was required, then the pilot engine would be coupled ahead of the train engine, irrespective of the power of this locomotive. The reason for the class 5 acting as pilot on this occasion was that she had not yet been fitted with a mechanical tablet catcher, whereas the class 2 was so equipped.

BATH JUNCTION —
COLLECTING THE SINGLE-LINE TABLET

19 "Let battle commence!" Class 7F, no.53806, in charge of the 11.00 a.m. down freight, is going great guns as she hits the start of the 1 in 50 climb out of Bath. The fireman is retrieving from the mechanical catcher, the single-line tablet which has been picked up on passing the Junction signal box.

18 All down trains, as they passed the Junction signal box, had to collect the tablet for the single-line section to Midford. Nearly all engines that worked regularly over the Somerset & Dorset, were equipped with a mechanical tablet catcher, but Southern class T9, no.30706, working the 7.5 p.m. Bath to Bournemouth, was not so fitted, and the fireman had to pick up the tablet by hand. This was done by means of the "Big pouch" — a normal tablet satchel attached to a large metal hoop — which the signalman held up for the fireman to collect by thrusting his arm through the hoop.

THE CLIMB OUT OF BATH

20 Whit Sunday 1956 had been a glorious summer's day. Several extra trains had run down to Bournemouth, and in the cool of the evening two class 2P, 4-4-0s, nos.40509 and 40700, are climbing the bank out of Bath on their way down to Evercreech Junction to assist two of the returning excursion trains over the Mendips. No.40509 was an ex-Midland class 2 with 7′0½″ coupled wheels, whilst no.40700 was one of the later L.M.S. built engines with coupled wheels of 6′9″.

21

The climb out of Bath, commenci immediately at 1 in 50 from Ba Junction, started with a lor sweeping curve turning throu nearly 180°, until the line w heading south east out of the city. O the evening of 22nd June, 1954, S & class 7F, 2-8-0 no.53807, in charge the 7.18 p.m. down goods, has ju passed the Midland bracket sigr which told drivers of up trai whether they had the road to run over the Midland main line, or t goods loop. Only a few da previously, no.53807 had arrived ba from Derby after a general overha which included the replacement her large boiler with one of 4′9½ diameter, and also the fitting of a n one-piece smokebox saddle.

22

B.R. Standard class 4, 2-6-4 tanks did not start to work over the Somerset & Dorset until November, 1963. In the spring of 1965, no.80134 is seen climbing towards Devonshire tunnel with the 1.10 p.m. down local, and has just passed underneath the footbridge which made a wonderful grandstand from which to watch trains entering and leaving the tunnel.

e 12.35 p.m. down goods comes up vards Devonshire tunnel, hauled by ge boilered S & D class 7F, 2-8-0 53806 and banked in the rear by a ss 4F, 0-6-0. A picture taken in ril, 1955, from above the northern rance to the tunnel.

DEVONSHIRE TUNNEL

In the climb out of Bath, the line passed through the narrow, and very restricted, bore of Devonshire tunnel which was just over a quarter of a mile long and on a rising gradient of 1 in 50. The tunnel had no ventilation shafts, and conditions on the footplate, particularly of the second engine of a double headed train, could be extremely unpleasant.

24 An interesting visitor to the Somerset & Dorset. S.R "Schools" class 4-4-0, no.30932 *Blundells*, with class 2P 4-4-0, no.40601, drifts downhill out of Devonshire tunnel on 25th April, 1954, with an enthusiasts' excursion. The "Schools" had been specially laid on to haul the train which had been organised by the Ian Allan Group.

25

"Two into one will go — just!" Class 3F, 0-6-0, no.43441 and S & D class 7F, 2-8-0, no.53807 climbing towards Devonshire tunnel with the 9.18 a.m. (SO) Birmingham to Bournemouth on 11th September, 1954. The clearance between the top of the chimney of a 7F and the roof of the tunnel was less than one foot!

26 S & D class 7F, 2-8-0, no.53810 toils up the 1 in 50 out of Devonshire tunnel into Lyncombe Vale with the 8.55 a.m. goods from Bath to Evercreech Junction. After a slow, laborious passage up through the tunnel, the relief for footplate crews, when their engine at last emerged into the fresh air of Lyncombe Vale, was tremendous.

27 The up "Pines Express", unusually hauled by two class 5 4-6-0 locomotives, drifts down the 1 in 50 through Lyncombe Vale on 31st March, 1956. The leading engine, no.73052, is a B.R. Standard class 5, whilst the train engine, no.44917, is an ex L.M.S. Stanier "Black Five". Both the B.R. Standard engine and the Stanier designed engine — from which the B.R. type was derived — gave outstanding service over the Somerset & Dorset and were universally liked by S & D enginemen.

LYNCOMBE VALE

After emerging from Devonshire tunnel, the line continued climbing south east at 1 in 50 through Lyncombe Vale for a further quarter of a mile, before plunging into Combe Down tunnel.

28 The 9.40 a.m.(SO) from Sheffield to Bournemouth, climbing through Lyncombe Vale in September, 1950. Class 2P, 4-4-0, no.40634 is assisting Ivatt class 4, 2-6-0, no.43036. The severity of the Somerset & Dorset route quickly sorted out the good from the indifferent in locomotive design. The Ivatt 2-6-0's proved to be poor steamers and — much to the relief of S & D enginemen, who had nicknamed the class "Doddlebugs" — they soon disappeared from the Somerset & Dorset scene.

29 With the end of the climb out of Bath in sight, class 2P, 4-4-0, no.40696 and S & D class 7F, 2-8-0, no.53804 approach Combe Down tunnel in June, 1957, with the 7.35 a.m. (SO) from Nottingham to Bournemouth.

30

Nearly all freight trains had to be assisted in the very difficult climb out of Bath, and were banked in the rear, the banking engine dropping off at this bridge just before the entrance to Combe Down tunnel, and then returning downhill to Bath Junction. Engines carrying out this banking duty, were protected by having picked up a special "Bath Bank Engine" staff on passing Bath Junction Box on the outward journey, and this was given up on arrival back at the Junction. On 6th October, 1956, however, S & D class 7F, 2-8-0, no.53807 had had no assistance and, by the time she reached this bridge, had been reduced to little more than walking pace in her efforts to lift the 12.35 p.m. freight out of Bath. But the struggle was almost over, for the entrance to Combe Down tunnel, and the end of the climb, were only a few yards away.

In June, 1957, B.R. class 5, 4-6-0, no.73051, assisted by a 4F, 0-6-0, is about to enter the tunnel with the 9.10 a.m. (SO) Birmingham to Bournemouth.

COMBE DOWN TUNNEL

This was the longest tunnel on the line, and ran for just over one mile under Combe Down to lead the Somerset & Dorset into open country south of Bath. From a few yards inside the northern entrance, the line descended southwards at 1 in 100. Like Devonshire tunnel, the bore was very restricted and had no ventilation shafts.

The down "Pines Express", hauled by class 2P, 4-4-0, no.40563 and Stanier "Black Five" no.44839, coming up through the wooded Lyncombe Vale towards Combe Down tunnel in May 1953.

33

A warm summer's evening in 1959. S & D class 7F, 2-8-0, no.53802 emerges from the northern end of Combe Down tunnel into the evening sunshine with the 4.45 p.m. up goods from Evercreech Junction.

34

The down "Pines Express", drawn by class 2P, 4-4-0, no.40634 and S.R. Pacific no.34043 *Combe Martin*, leaving the southern end of Combe Down tunnel in August 1954. No.40634 was one of a batch of L.M.S. standard class 2P, 4-4-0s built at Derby in 1928. Together with two other engines from the batch, she was allocated to the Somerset & Dorset where her original number was 45.

35 On a misty day in March, 1954, S.R. class U1, 2-6-0, no.31906, assisted by class 2P, 4-4-0 no.40563, climbs towards Combe Down tunnel with the 11.40 a.m. from Bournemouth. The U1 was being assessed for possible use over the Somerset & Dorset, and the train had been specially made up to twelve coaches for the test run.

HORSECOMBE VALE

From Combe Down tunnel, the Somerset & Dorset emerged into the lovely surroundings of Horsecombe Vale. The gradient now steepened to 1 in 55 down as the line descended towards Tucking Mill viaduct.

36

After emerging from Combe Down tunnel, S & D class 7F, 2-8-0, no.53807 is running smartly downhill through Horsecombe Vale with the 8.55 a.m. Bath - Evercreech Junction goods. Although the gradient is 1 in 55 down, the engine has steam on. Instructions to drivers were that on emerging from Combe Down tunnel, sufficient steam should be applied to keep the couplings well strained; the brief to the guard was to keep the brake well on until his van had passed Midford signal box. The fireman is inserting the tablet in the exchange apparatus ready to be given up at Midford at the end of the single line section from Bath Junction.

37 Class 2P, 4-4-0, no.40563 and S.R. Pacific no.34041 *Wilton*, coast down over Tucking Mill viaduct with the down "Pines" relief on 24th April, 1954.

TUCKING MILL VIADUCT

This fine and imposing viaduct, set in the wooded surroundings of Horsecombe Vale, carried the Somerset & Dorset on downhill towards Midford.

38

Eleven years later, on 31st March, 1965, B.R. 2-6-0, no.76027 passes over the viaduct with the 4.21 p.m. down semi-fast from Bath.

NEARING MIDFORD

After leaving Tucking Mill viaduct, the line curved south west through a short rock cutting and then swept on downhill towards Midford, passing, on the right, the tree-clustered grounds of Midford Castle and on the left, Midford's small goods yard. The yard's connection with the main line was by trailing points in the down direction controlled from a ground frame, "Midford A".

39 B.R. 2-6-0, no.76015 and class 9F, 2-10-0, no.92220 *Evening Star* running downhill past the grounds of Midford Castle with the 9.55 a.m. ex Bath on 1st September, 1962. *Evening Star*, the last steam locomotive to be built by British Railways, had been specially transferred to Bath Motive Power Depot on 8th August, 1962, so as to be able to work, on 8th September, 1962, the last "Pines Express" to run over the Somerset & Dorset.

40

Ex Midland class 2P, 4-4-0, no.405 pictured from the grounds of Midford Castle on a summer afternoon in July 1955, as she drifts down towards Midford with the 4.37 p.m. local from Bath to Templecombe.

41 On 25th July, 1953, S.R. Pacific no.34040 *Crewkerne*, coasts down past Midford goods yard with the 9.5 a.m. Bristol to Bournemouth. The front of the engine is just level with the small hut housing the ground frame, "Midford A", which controlled the entrance to the goods yard.

42 In the late afternoon of 23rd July, 1955, Stanier "Black Five" no.44859, in charge of the 2.45 p.m. (SO) Bournemouth to Bristol, climbs from Midford towards Combe Down tunnel. The second and third coaches are ex-L.N.E.R. articulated stock.

43

43
Between the goods yard and the station at Midford, the line passed underneath Tucking Mill lane. Officially, this spot was known as "The Long Arch Bridge", but it was more like a very short tunnel, being 37 yards long. On the ground above this little tunnel was sited the Midford down home signal and a backing signal (*see below*). Heading south, light engine, on 15th September, 1962, is ex L.M.S. Ivatt 2-6-2T no.41296.

MIDFORD

At Midford, the 4 mile single-line section from Bath Junction came to an end, the double line commencing two thirds of the way across Midford viaduct, and continuing for the next 32 miles as far as Templecombe. Midford station, situated on a narrow ledge cut into the steep hillside, was rather primitive by Somerset & Dorset standards. The one platform was on the west side of the line, and the buildings were of wooden construction.

44
The first up train of the day, the 7.00 a.m. ex Templecombe, arriving at Midford, hauled by class 4F, 0-6-0, no.44523. On the right is a backing signal which was used as follows. If, for example because of a poor steaming locomotive, the driver of an up freight decided there was a risk of stalling in Combe Down tunnel, he would bring his train to a stand before the tunnel entrance and use the lineside telephone to advise the Midford signalman of the situation. The signalman would then pull off the backing signals which authorised the driver to reverse downhill, passing the down home and starting signals at danger, and setting his train back onto the up road of the double line beyond the viaduct. What happened next is another story! The driver might decide to have another "go" (if his engine now had a full head of steam) but more often he would wait for an engine to be sent out from Bath to assist him up through the tunnel.

45

Midford signal box — like nearly all signal boxes on the Somerset & Dorset — was kept in immaculate condition. Signalman Percy Savage, who had 46 years railway service, is standing beside the Tyer Single-Line Tablet Instrument. Hanging on hooks on Percy's right, are some of the tablet carrying satchels which were used when tablets were exchanged by means of the Whitaker mechanical system. This was the normal method of tablet exchange, but if an engine was not fitted with a mechanical catcher, then the exchange had to be done by hand, and a "Big pouch" was used. Some "Big pouches" can be seen hanging above Percy's right shoulder.

46

0-6-0T, no.47557, returning in the rain from Bath to Radstock after a boiler wash-out, was not fitted with a mechanical catcher. Driver Charlie Rawlings is holding out the Bath Junction - Midford tablet contained in a "Big pouch", for signalman Percy Savage to take by hand.

47

The single-line from Bath Junction became double near the southern end of Midford viaduct. Class 4F 0-6-0, no.44417 bears left onto the down road with the 3.20 p.m. Bath - Templecombe local. Midford signal box, seen in the distance above the last coach, was unusual in having a flat roof, the result of rebuilding after being damaged in an accident in July, 1936.

MIDFORD VIADUCT

Just to the south of Midford station lay the eight-arch Midford viaduct which carried the Somerset & Dorset over the Bath road, the Cam brook, the Somersetshire Coal Canal, and the G.W.R. Limpley Stoke - Camerton branch, the track of which was lifted in 1958.

48

Class 2P 4-4-0, no.40564 and rebuilt S.R. Pacific no.34046 *Braunton* cross Midford viaduct on 27th August, 1960, in charge of the 9.25 a.m. (SO), Bournemouth to Manchester. On the left is the roof of the Hope & Anchor Inn, where more than one tablet had landed after being knocked out of the jaws of the mechanical catcher when the engine of a down train had rolled just at the vital moment of giving up the tablet! (The next move was for the signalman to go to the Hope & Anchor and ask "May we have our tablet back please?" — a situation that could have certain compensations, if the time of day was right.)

49

On a bitterly cold day early in 1965, B.R. 2-6-0 no.76013 leaves Midford viaduct with the 1.10 p.m. down local.

— AND SUMMER

50

The 10.28 a.m. (SO), Manchester to Bournemouth, hauled by class 4F, no.44417 and S.R. Pacific no.34099 *Lynmouth*, heads south from Midford on a warm afternoon in late summer, 1958. The small hut — seen in front of the leading coach — housed "Midford B" ground frame which controlled the siding in the foreground.

THE MIDFORD VALLEY

From Midford, the Somerset & Dorset r[un?]
south west towards Radstock through [the?]
Midford and Wellow valleys; the gradie[nt?]
undulated constantly, and reverse curv[es?]
followed one after the other in quick successi[on?]
as the line hugged the hillside. The reason f[or?]
the somewhat erratic path taken by t[he?]
Somerset & Dorset over this section, was th[at?]
when the line was built, it followed, as closely [as?]
possible, the course of an old plateway la[id?]
down at the turn of the 18th century to conv[ey?]
coal from the mines around Radstock, to t[he?]
canal system at Midford. This tramway, whi[ch?]
had been worked by horses, kept closely to t[he?]
side of the valleys and, following the contours [of?]
the land, abounded in curves. In some place[s?]
however, these curves became too severe f[or?]
even the Somerset & Dorset to follow!

51 The 7.45 a.m. (SO) Bradford to Bournemouth, hauled by class 2P, no.40563 and Stanier "Black Five" no.44945, passing Midford's majestic down advance starting signal in August 1950. Soon after the Western Region of British Railways had taken over the northern half of the Somerset & Dorset in 1958, this signal was replaced by a much shorter, commonplace, Western type.

52 On 11th July, 1953, class 2P, 4-4-0, no.40700 and S & D class 7F, 2-8-0, no.53801 come swinging through the reverse curves towards Midford with the 8.5 a.m. (SO), Bournemouth to Sheffield.

53

The down "Pines Express", hauled by class 2P, 4-4-0, no.40564 and B.R. class 5, no.73050, running south through the Midford valley in early spring, 1955.

n 20th June, 1959, class 2P, 4-4-0, .40697 and B.R. class no.73052 are ssing by on their way south with the 0 a.m. (SO), Birmingham to ournemouth. Coming north, class , 4-4-0, no.40700 and B.R. class 5, .73051 have been held at Midford's outer home signal with the 9.55 m. (SO), Bournemouth to Leeds, aiting for the down express to clear e Bath Junction - Midford single e section.

55 The up "Pines Express", hauled by class 2P, 4-4-0, no.40569 and B.R. class 5, no.73050, sweeping through the reverse curves near Lower Twinhoe in July, 1960.

THE MIDFORD VALLEY

56 21st August, 1960. Class 9F, 2-10-0, no.92203 is running south from Midford with the Sunday 9.30 a.m. — which only ran during the summer service — from Bath to Bournemouth. Happily, no.92203 has been preserved and is now owned by the artist, David Shepherd.

57

2P, 4-4-0, no.40697 — blowing off vigorously — and S.R. Pacific no.34041 "Wilton", drift slowly towards Midford on 28th August, 1954, with the 9.55 a.m. (SO) Bournemouth to Leeds. The Midford up distant signal had been on, and they were to be held at Midford up outer home signal for some ten minutes whilst a down train, running late, occupied the single-line section between Bath Junction and Midford.

58 On 5th August, 1950, class 2P, 4-4-0, no.40698 and class 4F, 0-6-0, no.43875 were held at Midford up outer home signal with the 12.25 p.m. relief Bournemouth to Birmingham, as the Bath Junction - Midford single-line section was not clear. But their delay was short lived, for no sooner had they come to a stand than the down "Pines Express" — which had been occupying the section — appeared round the corner.

WINTER IN THE MIDFORD VALLEY

Early in January, 1963, the South West of England was hit by some of the worst blizzards in living memory. The staff of the Somerset & Dorset fought a desperate battle to keep their line open, but further long and heavy falls of snow finally defeated all their efforts. High on the Mendip hills, massive drifts blocked the line, and several trains became marooned, buried deep in the snow. With great difficulty, the line from Bath as far as Midsomer Norton was kept open and trains carrying much needed coal continued to run.

59 The scene near Lower Twinhoe on 26th January, 1963, as B.R. 2-6-0, no.76029 ran towards Midford with the 6.25 a.m. up goods from Evercreen Junction. The snow was so deep that it took me nearly an hour to walk the mile from Midford station to the spot from which this picture was taken.

60 As S & D class 7F, 2-8-0, no.53807 drew near to Midford on 15th January, 1963, with a coal train from Norton Hill colliery, she was already steaming hard to get a good run at the steep climb up to Combe Down tunnel which lay ahead.

61 On a bitterly cold afternoon in early January, 1963, S & D 7F, 2-8-0, no.53808 is caught briefly by the weak winter sunshine as she plods south from Midford with a down goods.

THE WELLOW VALLEY

62 The down "Pines Express" running towards Wellow in early summer 1957, drawn by class 2P, 4-4-0, no.40569 and B.R. class 5, no.73049.

63

Class 2P, 4-4-0, no.40563, rounding a bend at speed, draws near to Wellow with the 3.20 p.m. down local. The track maintenance on the Somerset & Dorset was exemplary; although the line between Bath and Evercreech Junction abounded in curves, the riding was remarkably smooth.

64 S & D class 7F, 2-8-0, no.53807, in charge of the 1.5 p.m. up goods train from Evercreech Junction, starts blowing off as she drifts past Midford up distant signal at caution on 11th May, 1957. Ten minutes earlier, I could well have done with a similar signal when I had very nearly sat on an adder!

65 S & D class 4F, 0-6-0, no.44561 and B.R. class 5, no.73047 running towards Wellow with the 10.30 a.m. (SO) Liverpool to Bournemouth, on 18th July, 1959.

WELLOW

The village of Wellow was served by an attractive small station, similar in design and lay-out to the other stations on the Somerset & Dorset between Evercreech Junction and Bath.

66 Ex Midland 0-4-4T, no.58072 standing in the early evening sunshine at Wellow station on 25th April, 1955, with the 6.5 p.m. down local from Bath to Binegar.

67 S & D 7F, 2-8-0, no.53801 leaves the village of Wellow behind as she steams north east with an up goods on 25th March, 1961.

68 Drivers Bert Brewer and Donald Beale — in charge of Stanier "Black Five" no.44888 and S.R. Pacific no.34043 *Combe Martin* respectively — get a wave from my daughter Diana as they head south west from Wellow with a relief to the down "Pines Express" in early autumn, 1958.

WELLOW

69 Wellow viaduct, situated a ¼ mile to the east of Wellow station, carried the Somerset & Dorset over a small cleft in the hillside and also the Wellow - Hinton Charterhouse road. Crossing the viaduct on a warm evening in May, 1957, is the 7.5 p.m. down semi-fast from Bath to Bournemouth, hauled by B.R. class 4, 2-6-0, no.76068.

70 Between Radstock and Midford the Somerset & Dorset had followed, as closely as possible, the path of an old tramway which, in turn, had been laid along the towpath of a canal, constructed from Radstock to Midford, but never brought into use. The course of the canal bed can be seen on the right of this picture of S & D class 7F, 2-8-0, no.53801 nearing Wellow with an up goods train in early May, 1956.

SINGLE HILL

71 Two miles south west of Wellow, the Somerset & Dorset passed close to the village of Shoscombe, but no station had been provided for the local community until 1929. In that year, two short concrete platforms were erected and Shoscombe & Single Hill Halt was opened to the public on 23rd September. On a pleasant Sunday morning in early September, 1960, B.R. class 5, no.73087 is heading north east from Single Hill with the Sunday 9.45 a.m. Bournemouth to Bristol.

WRITHLINGTON

72 As the Somerset & Dorset approached Writhlington, one mile south west of Shoscombe, the farming country to the south of the line gave way to the first of the collieries surrounding Radstock. Passing Writhlington signal box — just before the heavens opened — is B.R. 2-6-4T, no.80059 in charge of the 3.20 p.m. down local from Bath.

73 Two class 3F 0-6-0T's, no.7496 (still with her pre-nationalisation number) and no.47465 standing outside Radstock shed on 25th February, 1950.

RADSTOCK

Radstock, 10½ miles south west of Bath, is in the heart of the North Somerset coalfields, and many of the collieries were connected to the Somerset & Dorset. It was also from Radstock that the Somerset & Dorset commenced the very difficult and arduous 7½ mile climb up the northern slopes of the Mendip hills to Masbury Summit, 811 feet above sea level. Engines were required for shunting the collieries, and also for banking goods trains up to Masbury Summit, so it was natural that there should be a small shed at Radstock to house the engines required for these duties.

74 Some colliery sidings at Radstock could only be reached after passing under Tyning's Bridge — known to S & D enginemen as the "Marble Arch" — which had the very limited clearance of only 10'10" from rail level to the roof of the arch. This precluded the use of any but the very smallest of locomotives. For many years the Somerset & Dorset had three delightful little engines which could pass underneath "Marble Arch", but sadly, these were scrapped in 1929 and replaced by two Sentinel four-wheeled steam shunters of unorthodox appearance. However, in the late 40s, one of the Sentinels was transferred elsewhere and Radstock received as a replacement, an attractive little engine — ex Lancashire & Yorkshire 0-4-0 saddle tank no.51202. She is seen standing outside Radstock shed — with the front end of an ex L.M.S. class 3F, 0-6-0T. towering above her!

75 The first appearance of a B.R. class 9F, 2-10-0 on the Somerset & Dorset. On Tuesday, 29th March, 1960, an event of great interest took place on the Somerset & Dorset — the trial of a class 9F, 2-10-0 to assess the suitability of this class for hauling passenger trains over the line. The locomotive on test, no.92204, was set to haul eleven bogies from Bath to Bournemouth and back, with no assistance being given for the climb over the Mendips. The weather on the day of the test run was appalling, with high wind and driving rain, but the locomotive, most ably handled by driver Bill Rawles and fireman Ron Bean, put up an outstanding performance. As a result, four class 9Fs, nos.92203/4/5 and 6 were allocated to Bath Motive Power Depot for the summer service, and their use reduced substantially the amount of double heading required.

76 Driver Bill Rawles, whose expert handling of no.92204 under very difficult conditions, resulted in the Somerset & Dorset being allocated 9Fs — probably the best locomotives the line ever had. (A picture taken on a rather sunnier occasion!)

THE START OF THE CLIMB OVER THE MENDIP HILLS

In addition to the Somerset & Dorset, Radstock was also served by the North Somerset line of the old Great Western Railway, the S & D and G.W. stations being almost side by side. Surprisingly, there was no direct connection between the two lines although, ironically, one was put in after the closure of the Somerset & Dorset to enable coal from Writhlington Colliery to be taken out over the G.W. line to Frome. Immediately to the west of the stations, both lines crossed the main Bath - Shepton Mallet road by adjacent level-crossings — the cause of monumental traffic jams on Saturdays in high summer! The Somerset & Dorset then commenced climbing immediately at 1 in 50, and in less than ½ mile had gained sufficient height to swing south-west over the top of the G.W. line. The climb over the Mendips was on with a vengeance.

77 A libellous picture of Somerset & Dorset class 7F, 2-8-0, no.53803! In this composite view of no.53803 starting the climb over the Mendips with a down goods train on a bitterly cold day in January, 1954, it looks as if she required banking assistance for eleven wagons and a brake van! The truth is that after taking the photograph on the left, some thirty wagons passed by before I took the second picture, on the right, of the class 3F, 0-6-0T banker at the rear of the train. The other class 3F, 0-6-0T, is returning downhill on the up line, after banking an earlier freight up to Masbury Summit. In the foreground is the ex Great Western North Somerset line, over the top of which the S & D train is about to pass.

78

Somerset & Dorset class 7F, 2-8-0, no.53803, again in charge of a down goods train, but this time on a fresh spring morning in April 1956. She has just crossed over the top of the G.W. North Somerset line and is climbing briskly up the 1 in 50 towards Midsomer Norton — with a class 3F, 0-6-0T, pushing away heartily in the rear.

79 A down evening goods train crosses over the Great Western line, half a mile west of Radstock. Officially, this location was known as the North Somerset Viaduct, but most S & D railwaymen always referred to it as the Five Arches.

MIDSOMER NORTON

Two miles of climbing from Radstock on a ruling gradient of 1 in 50 brought the Somerset & Dorset to Midsomer Norton station, set high on the hillside overlooking the town in the valley below. Through the station the gradient eased to 1 in 300, only to steepen again to 1 in 53 immediately after the platform end. To the south a small goods yard adjoined the station on the down side, whilst shortly before reaching the station, the line had passed Norton Hill Colliery, also on the down side. Midsomer Norton was an attractive little station built in the usual S & D style, and during the summer months, was always beautifully decked out with a profusion of flowers.

There used to be fierce competition on the Somerset & Dorset for the annual "Best kept station" award, which was for the best kept station — in every respect. Midsomer Norton, with its magnificent floral display, used to carry off the award year after year. But not, I recall, one year in the early 50s, which surprised me for I thought that their flowers had been even better than usual. On commenting about this to a station master down the line, his immediate reply was "Yes Mr. Peters, their flowers may well have been outstanding, but did you see the state of the brass in their lavatories?" This competition was a serious business on the Somerset & Dorset.

80 Class 2P, 4-4-0, no.40634 and B.R. class 5, no.73050 struggle up through Midsomer Norton station with the down "Pines Express" as a snow storm breaks over the Mendips in February, 1955.

82 In August, 1955, Bath Motive Power Depot had the misfortune to be landed with a supply of foreign coal and whilst it lasted, S & D firemen — try as they might — were unable to prevent their engines laying voluminous clouds of thick brown smoke over the countryside! Ex Midland 2P, 4-4-0, no.40527 — from Templecombe shed and burning British coal — is assisting "Black Five" no.44963 as they climb uphill at 1 in 50 towards Midsomer Norton station with the 10.30 a.m. (SO) Liverpool to Bournemouth on 6th August.

81 The 11.00 a.m. down freight from Bath, hauled by S & D class 7F, no.53807 and banked in the rear by class 3F, 0-6-0T, no.47557, passing through Midsomer Norton station in July, 1960. Standing on the up road beside the signal box is another 0-6-0T, no.47275, her shunting operations temporarily suspended whilst the freight passed through.

MIDSOMER NORTON

83 The Somerset & Dorset handled a considerable amount of pigeon traffic, and more often than not these special trains were entrusted to the S & D class 7F, 2-8-0's. Coming up to Midsomer Norton station on an overcast day in May, 1960 is no.53806 in charge of an eleven bogie pigeon special from Crewe to Templecombe.

The signals on the Somerset & Dorset were of three main types. 1) Original S & D signals with a wooden post and ball-and-spike finial. 2) Signal arms, either of S & D or S.R. pattern, mounted on a post made of two old rails bolted together. 3) L & S.W.R. type lattice posts with either L & S.W.R. lower-quadrant or S.R. upper-quadrant arms. The up starter on the left has an L & S.W.R. lattice post and an S.R. upper-quadrant arm.

84

In 1958 the Western Region gained a dominating control over the Somerset & Dorset. Two manifestations of this change in control were the dwindling size of goods trains as freight traffic was diverted away from the line, and the arrival of ex-G.W. locomotives as replacements for exL.M.S. types. In the autumn of 1963 ex-G.W.R. 0-6-0, no.2291 pauses briefly beside Midsomer Norton signal box with an up freight of four wagons.

85   The National Coal Board used one of their own locomotives at Norton Hill for shunting the colliery yard. From 1953 the engine engaged in this work was *Lord Salisbury*, an 0-6-0 saddle tank built by Peckett in 1906. *Lord Salisbury* was not allowed onto the main line, but is seen here standing adjacent to the Somerset & Dorset line as class 7F, no.53810 passed by with an up freight.

86   S & D class 7F, 2-8-0, no.53809 and class 3F, 0-6-0T, no.47557 standing side by side at the entrance to Norton Hill Colliery.

CHILCOMPTON TUNNEL

After easing briefly to 1 in 300 through Midsomer Norton station, the gradient steepened again to 1 in 53 as the Somerset & Dorset continued to climb higher and higher up the Mendips. As far as possible, the line followed the lie of the land in the climb, but about ¾ mile short of Chilcompton, a bluff in the hillside necessitated a short tunnel. Chilcompton tunnel, 66 yards long, had separate bores for the up and down roads — a reminder that the Somerset & Dorset was originally built as a single line, and later doubled.

87 From Midsomer Norton up to Chilcompton tunnel was one, long, hard slog. The gradient the whole way was a relentless 1 in 53 and as the down "Pines Express" approached the tunnel on 4th July, 1953, the train engine, Stanier "Black Five" no.44826, must have been working close to her maximum, judging by the wonderfully exhilarating sound she was making. The pilot engine, class 2P, no.40505, was also working hard, but the softer bark of the elderly ex Midland engine was almost drowned by the efforts of the class 5.

89 The down "Pines Express" again, but on this ▶ occasion — 28th May, 1949 — the pilot engine, 2P, 4-4-0, no.569, was doing most of the work. As the train emerged slowly from the tunnel it was obvious that Horwich "Crab" no.2754, was very much "off beat" — and with steam oozing from all sorts of places where it shouldn't have done!

88 Class 2P, 4-4-0, no.40634 and rebuilt S.R. Pacific no.34028 *Eddystone* about to enter the tunnel with the down "Pines Express" on 2nd July, 1960.

90 In bright evening sunlight late in April, 1955, the 6.5 p.m. Bath - Binegar local comes up out of the tunnel, drawn by 0-4-4T, no.58072, an "elderly lady" built for the Midland Railway by Neilson & Co. in 1893.

CHILCOMPTON TUNNEL

91

B.R. class 5, no.73051 was making an excellent climb of the Mendips on Whit Monday 1965, as she burst out of Chilcompton tunnel with an eight coach excursion from Bath to Bournemouth.

92

Running fast downhill, a pair of class 2P, 4-4-0s, nos.40601 and 40697 leave the tunnel on their descent towards Midsomer Norton with an up local in July 1953. No.40601 was working back to Bath after assisting a down express over the Mendips earlier in the day.

CHILCOMPTON

Up to Chilcompton tunnel the gradient had been 1 in 53, but after leaving the tunnel the climb — following a very brief easing — became even more severe, steepening to 1 in 50 and culminating in a very difficult stretch where the line curved upwards through a rock cutting to reach Chilcompton station. On days when the mists came down, and low cloud enveloped the Mendips, many a driver had an anxious moment as his engine laboured up through this cutting. As at Midsomer Norton, the gradient was eased to 1 in 300 through Chilcompton station, only to revert immediately to 1 in 50 beyond the platform.

93 S & D class 7F, 2-8-0, no.53801 — one of the 1914 series — comes up through Chilcompton with the 8.55 a.m. Bath - Evercreech Junction freight on a cold, frosty morning in November, 1957.

94 A sad occasion — the final run of the last surviving S & D class 7F, 2-8-0, no.53807, one of the reboilered 1925 series. The end came on Saturday, 5th September, 1964. No.53807 had worked the 11 a.m. goods from Bath to Evercreech Junction, and then made her last run home, engine and brake. She is seen here passing through Chilcompton station.

95 S & D class 7F, 2-8-0, no.53808 — one of the large-boilered 1925 series — and S.R. Pacific no.34095 *Brentor*, climbing hard south of Chilcompton with the 7.35 a.m. (SO) Nottingham to Bournemouth on 23rd August, 1952.

96 Two S & D class 7F, 2-8-0s appearing in double-harness on a passenger train was a very rare sight. Nos.53804 and 53802 (both 1914 series engines), with their combined tractive effort of 70592 lb., were making light work of the eleven coach 7.35 a.m. (SO) Nottingham to Bournemouth as they came romping up towards Chilcompton rock cutting on 4th July, 1959.

MOOREWOOD

By the time Moorewood had been reached, the Somerset & Dorset had passed the 700′ contour and the worst of the climb was over. There were still 2½ miles to go to the summit, but the gradient now eased off to 1 in 67 as the line turned south towards Binegar.

97 S & D class 7F, 2-8-0, no.53810 — one of the re-boilered 1925 series — and B.R. class 4, 4-6-0, no.75072 climbing towards Moorewood on 3rd August 1957 with the 10.28 a.m. (SO) Manchester to Bournemouth express.

98 Unusual pairing of locomotives was always an interesting feature of the Somerset & Dorset, but this was a rare combination. Great Western Collett 0-6-0 no.3215 and Southern Bulleid Pacific no.34043 ''Combe Martin'' are heading north past Moorewood up distant signal with the 12.20 p.m. (SO) Bournemouth to Nottingham on 8th September 1962.

99 On Sunday, 12 January, 1958, considerable engineering work had been taking place in the vicinity of Moorewood. Ex L.M.S. class 4F, 0-6-0, no.44096 was standing beside Moorewood signal box — having been on the job since early morning — when, around midday, ex S & D class 4F, 0-6-0, no.44558 arrived to relieve no.44096 and her crew.

100 Two B.R. Standard 4-6-0s, class 4, no.75072 and class 5, no.73019, in charge of an excursion from Cheltenham to Bournemouth, nearing Moorewood on Whit Sunday 1960.

CLIMBING TOWARDS BINEGAR   101

1960 — THE TRIAL. On Tuesday, 29th March, 1960, in appalling weather conditions, a class 9F, 2-10-0 worked a test train from Bath to Bournemouth and back to assess the suitability of this class for hauling passenger trains over the Somerset & Dorset. I had already photographed the train leaving Bath, and at Radstock, and some quick motoring produced this third picture as no.92204, battling through the wind and rain, climbed towards Binegar with her eleven coach test train.

102

1962 — THE CULMINATION. On Saturday, 8th September, 1962, class 9F, 2-10-0, no.92220 *Evening Star*, worked, unassisted, the last "Pines Express" to run over the Somerset & Dorset. The 9F, expertly handled by driver Peter Guy and fireman Ronald Hyde, worked the heavy twelve coach train over the Mendips with consummate ease, giving final proof of what excellent locomotives they could have been for the Somerset & Dorset. But it was too late. With all through traffic diverted away from the line, the fate of the Somerset & Dorset was already sealed.

In this picture, the train is about to pass Binegar down distant signal which has an upper quadrant arm on a post made from two old rails bolted together. On the left, Moorewood's up distant signal has a lower quadrant arm and an L.S.W.R. lattice post.

103 On a glorious day in May, 1960, S & D class 7F, 2-8-0, no.53807 is heading south from Moorewood towards Binegar with an enthusiasts excursion organised by the Ian Allan Group.

104 Ex L.M.S. class 8F, 2-8-0s were only used occasionally on passenger trains over the Somerset & Dorset. On a crisp morning in early Autumn 1963, no.48737 is nearing Binegar with the 8.15 a.m. down local from Bath. Lacking the necessary equipment to steam heat her train, the 8F was probably not too popular with her passengers.

BINEGAR

From Moorewood, a further 1¼ miles of climbing brought the line up to the village of Binegar where there was a pleasant small station of typical Somerset & Dorset design. With only a little over one more mile of 1 in 63 and 1 in 73 to go, the long climb from Radstock up to Masbury Summit, 811 feet above sea level, was almost over.

105 S & D class 7F, 2-8-0, no.53804 — one of the 1914 series — and class 2P, 4-4-0, no.40700 arriving at Binegar with an up local in July 1953. The 7F had taken a freight from Bath down to Evercreech Junction in the early morning and, with no return working, was coupled ahead of the 2P to save a separate path having to be found for her to run back, light engine.

106

On 2nd August, 1952, a relief to the up "Pines Express" stopped at Binegar to detach class 3F, 0-6-0, no.43204 which had assisted S.R. Pacific no.34041 *Wilton* in the climb from Evercreech Junction up to Masbury Summit. The 3F — built for the Somerset & Dorset in 1896 — had set back onto the down road to allow the Pacific to proceed on her way again. Shortly afterwards, the 0-6-0 also departed, tender first, for Evercreech Junction.

107

Class 2P, 4-4-0, no.40601 and S & D class 7F, 2-8-0, no.53807 — one of the large-boilered 1925 series — departing from Binegar in the early morning of 16th September, 1950 with the 6.55 a.m. down local from Bath.

108

In 1956 British Railways decided to produce an instructional film on Emergency Single-line Working. Because, after the end of the summer service, no trains ran on Sundays between Bath and Evercreech Junction, the Somerset & Dorset was selected for the making of the film, and this took place on Sundays in late September and October. As the film was intended for showing throughout British Railways, great care was taken to prevent it from being identified with any particular Region. Shepton Mallet and Binegar, the two stations which appeared in the film, both had their names changed; Shepton Mallet became "Averton Hammer" and Binegar, "Boiland". The first two Sundays were devoted to filming scenes involving passenger train working. The engines used were B.R. Standard class 4 and class 5, 4-6-0s — types which could have been seen anywhere on British Railways. On the third Sunday it was the turn for shooting the freight scenes. Imagine my huge joy therefore, when the train came into view hauled by one of the highly individual S & D class 7F, 2-8-0s — and bearing the S & D headlamp code for a goods train! In this picture Mr. Fairbairn, Director of the B.T.C. Film Unit, is giving some instructions to the driver and pilotman, whilst the new sign board is ready to change Binegar signal box into "Boiland Signal Box".

109 Sunday, 6th January, 1963. S & D class 7F, 2-8-0s, nos.53809 and 53807 with the rear part of the previous Thursday's 3.30 a.m. down goods which they had just succeeded in retrieving from a tremendous drift near Winsor Hill, where the train had been buried for the last three days. Later three engines, approaching from the south, had managed to reach the front part of the train which they had then taken down to Evercreech Junction.

BINEGAR — IN DEEP WINTER

On 29th December, 1962, it began snowing heavily and as the New Year came in, some of the worst blizzards in living memory swept the south west of England. High up on the Mendips, conditions grew steadily worse until on Thursday, 3rd January, the Somerset & Dorset was finally overwhelmed, blocked completely by massive drifts. Several trains had become marooned in the snow and one, the 3.30 a.m. down goods, was lost for several hours, buried deep in drifts near Winsor Hill. The staff of the S & D made tremendous efforts to re-open their line, but it was not until three days later, on Sunday, 6th January, that one line was eventually cleared between Binegar and Shepton Mallet allowing single-line working to be initiated over this section. (The very section that, six years earlier, British Railways had used for the making of their film on Emergency Single-Line Working.)

110 The snow was so deep between the platforms that it had to be dug out by hand before the plough engines could pass through on their way to try and clear the up line over Masbury Summit. Class 7F, no.53809 is standing on the down line which had been cleared as far as Winsor Hill.

111 The plough engine, class 3F, 0-6-0T, no.47496, and her assistant, class 8F, 2-8-0, no.48660, standing at Binegar on Sunday, 6th January, after successfully clearing the up line between Midsomer Norton and Binegar.

112 Looking back from the plough engine at the class 8F, pushing for all her worth, as the pair forced their way up past Moorewood whilst endeavouring to clear the up line between Midsomer Norton and Binegar.

MASBURY SUMMIT

The culmination of the Somerset & Dorset's climb over the Mendips was at Masbury Summit, 811 feet above sea level. The approach from the north was at a comparatively mild 1 in 73 which was followed by a few brief yards on the level before the line, curving to the south west, started to descend steeply at 1 in 50 through a rock cutting.

113

On a glorious day in September 1961, the crews of class 2P, 4-4-0, no.40634 and S.R. Pacific no.34041 *Wilton* had no worries as they forged their way up the 1 in 50 through the rock cutting towards the Summit with the 9.25 a.m. (SO) Bournemouth to Manchester. But on damp and misty days, or when a light drizzle was falling, things could be very different, and to negotiate this stretch without stalling, called for enginemanship of a high order.

114 This gradient post at Masbury Summit marked the start of the Somerset & Dorset's eight mile, headlong descent down the southern slopes of the Mendips. In summer, wild flowers abounded in the cuttings and on the embankments of the Somerset & Dorset. At Masbury Summit there was also a particularly luscious patch of wild strawberries — which I liked to think was known only to the local gangers and myself!

115 Two class 4F 0-6-0s, nos.44561 and 44557 — both built for the Somerset & Dorset in 1922 by Armstrong Whitworth & Co. — coming up to the summit on 3rd September, 1955 with the 10.38 a.m. (SO) Manchester to Bournemouth.

116 The Summit at last! The 28th July, 1951, was a sultry, oppressive day and for the firemen of class 2P, no.40564 and class 7F, no.53805 — hauling a heavy, twelve coach, Nottingham - Bournemouth Relief — the climb from Radstock must have been a hot, tiring and long 7½ miles. So doubtless it was with more than the usual relief that they saw the summit coming into view. Now, for the next 8 miles, they could take things easy as their train swept downhill towards Evercreech Junction.

MASBURY SUMMIT

117 S & D class 7F, 2-8-0, no.53806 — one of the large-boilered 1925 series — approaching the Summit in May 1953 with the 4.5 p.m. down coal train from Midsomer Norton. The train was banked in the rear by class 3F, 0-6-0T, no.47496 which dropped off as soon as her driver had seen the rear brakevan pass safely over the summit. The banker then returned direct to Binegar, "wrong line", a procedure made possible by the driver having picked up a "bank engine staff" from the tablet-exchange apparatus as he had passed through Binegar earlier at the rear of the train.

118

The guard's view from a down freight as the banker, class 3F, 0-6-0T, no.47557, drops off at the Summit.

0

asbury Station, situated ¼ mile down from
e summit on the southern side, did not follow
e usual pattern for Somerset & Dorset
ations on the Bath Extension. On the up
atform — which had no canopy — a small
one building housed the booking office and
iting room. A little further down the
atform stood the signal box and then the
ationmaster's house — complete with bay
ndow. A small wooden shelter graced the
wn platform. Through the station the
adient eased to 1 in 300 — as at Midsomer
orton and Chilcompton — but this was too
ief to be of much help to S & D class 7F,
.53806, one of the large-boilered 1925 series,
she came plodding uphill on a hot afternoon
August 1953 with the 12.20 p.m. (SO) relief,
urnemouth to Walsall, made up of ten
-L.N.E.R. coaches. This heavy stock, filled to
pacity, would have been well over the
aximum load of 310 tons laid down for an S &
class 7F to take over Masbury Summit
assisted.

119 After 8 miles of climbing, much of it at 1 in 50, many locomotives would have been
feeling somewhat "winded" — but not class 9F 2-10-0 no.92001, which started blowing
off furiously as she entered the rock cutting for the final few yards up to the summit with
the 9.55 a.m. (SO) Bournemouth to Leeds. The 9Fs were outstanding locomotives,
capable of putting up a phenomenal performance in the hands of an experienced driver
— but to get the best out of a 9F also called for skill and phenomenal hard work on the
part of the fireman.

WINSOR HILL TUNNEL

From Masbury Summit the Somerset & Dorset immediately started to descend steeply, and over the next 3½ miles, as far as Shepton Mallet, the gradient hardly varied from 1 in 50 down. Two miles south of Masbury Summit the line passed through Winsor Hill Tunnel, the up and down lines having separate bores, another reminder that the Bath Extension of the Somerset & Dorset was originally constructed as a single line. When the Shepton Mallet - Binegar section was doubled in 1892, it was decided to deviate a short distance to the west at Winsor Hill so that the tunnel for the new (up) line could be 110 yards shorter than the original tunnel. The length of the old tunnel, used by the down line, was 242 yards, whereas the new tunnel was only 132 yards long.

121

The fireman's view from class 8F, 2-8-0, no.48737, in charge of an up freight in September 1964, as his engine is about to veer away from the down line in the climb up to the tunnel.

122 Class 2P, 4-4-0, no.40634 and S.R. Pacific no.34041 *Wilton* coming swiftly downhill towards Winsor Hill tunnel with the down "Pines Express" on 2nd October, 1954. Standing between the up and down lines is Winsor Hill signal box — the only box on the Somerset & Dorset to be built entirely of stone — which controlled the sidings leading into the quarries situated on either side of the line. A tall, corrugated iron clad, stone crushing plant in the quarry beside the up line, marred the beauty of the surrounding Mendip countryside.

123 Class 9F 2-10-0, no.92212 coasting downhill from the tunnel with the 9.35 a.m. (SO) Sheffield to Bournemouth in August 1961. The catch points on the up line were strategically placed to deal with any break-aways from goods trains toiling up the long stretch of 1 in 50.

124 An S & D class 7F, 2-8-0 in full cry. No.53807 — one of the 1925 series rebuilt with a smaller diameter boiler — climbing hard towards the tunnel with the 10.40 a.m. (SO) Exmouth to Cleethorpes on 26th August 1961.

SHEPTON MALLET

The Somerset & Dorset, continuing to descend southwards, came sweeping downhill at 1 in 50 towards Shepton Mallet, set in a fold in the southern slopes of the Mendips. Just before reaching the town, the line veered south east, crossing over first the six, 62′ high, arches of Bath Road viaduct, and then the much longer Charlton viaduct of twenty seven arches, before arriving at the station.

126

125 Charlton viaduct, 317 yards long, had 27 arches and was built on a curve. It also had the intriguing feature that halfway across, the gradient changed from 1 in 55 down to 1 in 55 up. On 16th April, 1955, the driver of S & D class 7F, no.53802, in charge of an up freight, had taken full advantage of the dip down to the middle of the viaduct to get up as much speed as possible before hitting the up grade and the long, hard climb that lay ahead up to Masbury Summit.

Class 2P, 4-4-0, no.40564 and B.R. class 5, no.73116, after a high speed descent from Masbury Summit with the 7.47 a.m. (SO) Bradford to Bournemouth, have left Charlton viaduct and are preparing to stop at Shepton Mallet station. The date was 30th August, 1958.

127 The station at Shepton Mallet followed the usual, neat, style built by the Somerset & Dorset on the Bath Extension. The main buildings were on the up side, whilst on the down platform there was a small waiting room and also the signalbox. Running in on 28th November, 1953, in low winter sunshine, is the 1.10 p.m. down local from Bath, hauled by class 2P, 4-4-0, no.40698.

128 *Evening Star* leaves Shepton Mallet on 13th September, 1963 with the 3.40 p.m. up from Bournemouth. In August 1962, class 9F, no.92220 *Evening Star* had been specially transferred to Bath Motive Power Depot to work the last "Pines Express" to run over the Somerset & Dorset. After the 1962 summer service had ended, all long distance and through trains were diverted away from the line, and the Somerset & Dorset passenger service became a purely local affair between Bath and Bournemouth. It was, therefore, somewhat surprising when, in August 1963, *Evening Star* was again transferred to the Somerset & Dorset, to while away her time hauling three and four coach trains between Bath and Bournemouth. *Sic transit gloria!*

129

Whilst the 7.43 a.m. (SO) Birmingham to Bournemouth was standing in Shepton Mallet station on 23rd July, 1955, the crew of S & D class 7F, no.53809 took the opportunity to top up their engine's water supply.

SHEPTON MALLET

130

Nearly all down goods trains were scheduled to stop at Shepton Mallet to take water. On 21st April, 1956, S & D class 7F, no.53803, in charge of the 12.35 p.m. down goods from Bath, was having her tender replenished, when sister engine no.53810 came thundering through with an up goods, gathering all the speed she could on the brief downhill stretch, before tackling the final, gruelling, 3½ miles, nearly all at 1 in 50, up to Masbury Summit.

131

On a hot afternoon in late summer 1961, B.R. class 4, 4-6-0, no.75027 and rebuilt S.R. Pacific no.34028 *Eddystone* get the 10.38 a.m. (SO) Manchester to Bournemouth under way again after a brief scheduled stop at Shepton Mallet.

132

But the sun did not always shine at Shepton Mallet! B.R. class 4 4-6-0, no.75023 and rebuilt S.R. Pacific, no.34046 *Braunton* running in, in pouring rain, with the up "Pines Express" on 6th August, 1962. Behind the first coach can just be seen the roof of Shepton Mallet's goods shed, beyond which was a spacious goods yard.

133

Two S & D class 7F, 2-8-0s on one passenger train was a rare sight — but this scene at Shepton Mallet in the late afternoon of 11th September, 1954, was not quite what it appeared to be. The train which nos.53807 and 53805 were hauling was, in fact, an up empty stock from Bournemouth.

134 As class 4F, 0-6-0, no.44422 and B.R. class 4, 4-6-0, no.75072 approached Shepton Mallet on the 23rd August, 1958 with the 10.5 a.m. (SO) Bournemouth to Cleethorpes, they were nearing the end of the first part of the climb over the Mendips. Once they had passed underneath this bridge — which carried a minor road over the S & D — there was a brief "breather" as the line dipped down through Shepton Mallet, before the second stage of the climb up to Masbury Summit had to be tackled.

135

Class 2P, 4-4-0, no.40569 and S & D class 4F, 0-6-0, no.44561 climbing past Prestleigh towards Shepton Mallet with a heavy twelve coach Relief from Bournemouth to Walsall on 1st August, 1953.

SOUTH OF SHEPTON MALLET

After leaving Shepton Mallet station, the Somerset & Dorset, climbing briefly, passed underneath the old G.W. East Somerset line from Witham to Wells, and then recommenced the dramatic descent of the Mendips, sweeping downhill for mile after mile at 1 in 50.

136 On Saturday 12th August, 1950, traffic was so heavy that nearly every engine that could turn a wheel had to be pressed into service. Radstock shed sent 0-6-0T, no.7316 down to Evercreech Junction to assist Ivatt 2-6-0, no.43036 in the climb over the Mendips with a northbound relief from Bournemouth. The pair are seen here climbing past Prestleigh in the rain.

137 Over three miles of 1 in 50 lay behind class 2P, no.40700 and B.R. class 5, no.73051 as they plodded up the last half mile of the long climb from Evercreech Junction towards Shepton Mallet with the 10.35 a.m. (SO) Bournemouth to Manchester in late summer 1958.

PRESTLEIGH VIADUCT

As the Somerset & Dorset followed a gently curving descent over open hillside towards Evercreech, the line passed over Prestleigh viaduct, a graceful structure of eleven arches.

138 S & D class 7F, 2-8-0, no.53808 and Stanier "Black Five" no.45332 climbing north from Prestleigh viaduct with the 2.45 p.m. (SO) Bournemouth to Bristol on 30th August, 1958.

139
The guard's view as S & D class 7F, 2-8-no.53805 takes a heavy freight steadily downh over Prestleigh viaduct. The S & D 7Fs were n only excellent locomotives for hauling hea freights up hill but, equally important, they h outstanding brake power to control the desce of their trains on the Somerset & Dorset's lo downhill stretches of 1 in 50. Just how difficu it was to match the S & D 7Fs' brakii qualities was brought home in 1959 when t Western Region tried out several types locomotives to replace the ageing S & D 7F Some of the results were most exciting!

140 Class 4F, 0-6-0, no.44561 (built for the S & D in 1922) passing over Prestleigh viaduct as she made her way laboriously up the southern slopes of the Mendips with an Evercreech Junction — Bath goods in April 1955.

141 The first test run of a B.R. class 4, 2-6-0 over the Somerset & Dorset was on 5th March, 1955. A week later, on 12th March, no.76027 was put in charge of the 12.55 p.m. ex Bournemouth, and is seen here coming up over Prestleigh viaduct.

142 B.R. class 9F, 2-10-0, no.92214 climbing away from Evercreech New in the early evening with the 3.40 p.m. up from Bournemouth.

EVERCREECH

The original Somerset Central Railway station built to serve the village of Evercreech, was almost two miles from this community. When construction of the Bath Extension of the Somerset & Dorset commenced in 1872, the new line passed right by the western edge of the village, so it was not surprising that a new station should be built for Evercreech. Initially, this was called Evercreech Village, but early on the name was changed to Evercreech New, although in 1888 the station was still being referred to officially as Evercreech Village. Meanwhile, on the opening of the Bath Extension, the original Somerset Central station for Evercreech became Evercreech Junction.

143

Over the years, I had the good fortune to be granted the occasional footplate permit. On the majority of these trips the weather was reasonable, but for the run I had on class 8F, 2-8-0, no.48737 with the 11.00 a.m. down goods on 15th September, 1964, the heavens opened and it poured with rain the whole way from Bath down to Evercreech Junction. As class 8F, no.48737 descended towards Evercreech New with her train, she met B.R. 2-6-4T, no.80081 coming up the bank with the 11.46 a.m. from Bournemouth.

144

S & D class 7F, 2-8-0, no.53809 coming up to Evercreech New on a really lovely, crisp Autumn morning in 1962. After working the 8.55 a.m. goods from Bath down to Evercreech Junction, there had been no return load for the 7F, so she was running back up to Bath, engine and brake.

145 Another of the excellent "Rail Tour" specials organised by the Ian Allan Group. The S & D class 7F, 2-8-0s were always a popular choice of motive power for hauling these excursion trains when they ran over the Somerset & Dorset. On 22nd September, 1962, no.53808 — now happily preserved by the Somerset & Dorset Railway Circle — is about to pass through Evercreech New with her nine coach special, in the early stages of the climb northwards over the Mendips. The gradient up to Evercreech New was 1 in 50, but as at Midsomer Norton, Chilcompton and Masbury, this was eased to 1 in 300 through the station, only for the 1 in 50 to set in again immediately afterwards.

EVERCREECH JUNCTION

From Evercreech New the line, now running south west, continued to descend at 1 in 50. Then after half a mile, the gradient at last began to ease as the branch from Burnham-on-Sea could be seen approaching on a straight run in from the north west. Just before the branch came in on a trailing connection, the main line turned south east through a very sharp curve and then dropped down the final ¼ mile into the Station. The crossing of the Mendips was over.

146 Ex G.W.R., 0-6-0, no.3218 running in past Evercreech Junction North Box with the afternoon milk train from Bason Bridge to Templecombe. As the train comes off the branch, the fireman is handing the single-line token to the signalman. The main line, curving round very sharply, can just be seen on the right hand side of the picture.

147 The 3.20 p.m. down local from Bath, hauled by class 4F, no.44422, drifts round the very sharp curve by the North Box, before dropping down the final ¼ mile into the Junction station. On the right is one of the S & D backing signals, used during shunting operations to authorise a driver to draw back on the down line, and then onto the branch, a freight train which had arrived from Bath.

EVERCREECH JUNCTION

There were three goods yards at Evercreech Junction, the principal yard being on the up side of the main line between the station and the North Box. A down yard lay on the east side of the branch shortly after it had left the main line, and there was also a small yard, complete with goods shed, adjacent to the station on the down side. Considerable activity took place in the main yards, at which all freight trains were scheduled to stop. As many freight trains either terminated or set off from these yards, provision was made for turning engines, a 56' turntable being situated in the "V" between the main line and the branch. This was long enough to turn an S & D class 7F but not a B.R. class 9F, which was one reason why these locomotives were only used on passenger trains which ran between Bath and Bournemouth (where they could be turned on the Branksome triangle).

148 14th February, 1954. S & D class 7F, no.53807 — one of the large-boilered 1925 series — is being turned, whilst standing on the left is sister engine no.53804, one of the 1914 series.

149 Class 3F, 0-6-0, no.43419 engaged in shunting the up yard on 8th August, 1953.

EVERCREECH JUNCTION

All northbound trains of over eight coaches — unless hauled by an S & D class 7F or a B.R. class 9F — had to be assisted in the climb over the Mendips, which began at Evercreech Junction. Prior to 1960, when Bath Motive Power Depot was first allocated 9Fs, one of the most enthralling sights to be seen on the Somerset & Dorset, used to occur at Evercreech Junction on Saturday mornings at the height of the summer service. From just after 10 a.m. engines would start arriving and lining up in the middle road. Some had assisted down trains over the Mendips earlier in the morning and after being

150 The line-up of assistant engines in the middle road on a Saturday morning in high summer. On 2nd August, 1958, all the assistant engines were class 2P, 4-4-0s, which was unusual as generally there would be at least one class 4F, 0-6-0 in the line up. On this occasion the engines were nos.40563, 40568, 40700, 40564 and 40697.

turned on the turntable by the North Box, would come backing down into the station. Others, coupled in twos and sometimes threes, would arrive, light engine, from Templecombe. Shortly before the first of the procession of up expresses was due, five assistant engines would be ready, waiting buffer to buffer, in the middle road.

151

As soon as an up express had come to a stand, the station foreman gave the bell code to the signalman and the points would be changed to allow the assistant engine to draw forward onto the main line, and then set back onto the train engine. The complete movement would be carried out quickly and with precision and, in the case of the up "Pines Express", would often be completed in less than three minutes — the time this train was booked to stop at the Junction. The whole operation was a model of staff co-operation and efficient working. On 21st July, 1951, the driver of class 2P, no.40568 was setting back carefully onto Stanier "Black Five" no.44839, with the fireman waiting, reading to couple up as soon as the buffers touched. The up "Pines Express" was on her way again very shortly afterwards.

On Saturday, 12th July, 1952, traffic was exceptionally heavy, and several of the S & D class 7F, 2-8-0s had been pressed into service for hauling some of the many extra trains being run. Early in the afternoon, class 7F, no.53800 ran in with a heavy twelve coach relief from Bournemouth to the North, and class 2P, no.40697 was quickly coupled ahead of her for the climb over the Mendips. When the "right away" was given, both engines were blowing off furiously as if eager to go, but the fireman of the 2P was still in the process of transferring the reporting number from the 7F to the front of his own engine — whilst the fireman of the 7F was leaning out, trying to see what was causing the brief delay.

153 After stopping for assistance, the 9.55 a.m. (SO) Bournemouth to Leeds sets off from the Junction on 16th September, 1950, hauled by class 2P, 4-4-0, no.569 and Ivatt class 4, 2-6-0 no.43036. Bearing in mind the Ivatt 2-6-0s' reputation on the Somerset & Dorset for poor steaming, it was probable that the 2P would be doing the major part of the work before many miles had been covered in the climb over the Mendips.

154

On a glorious afternoon in July, 1964, B.[
class 4, 2-6-0, no.76027, running in to t[
Junction with the 1.10 p.m. up local fro[
Bournemouth, is about to pass over the lev[
crossing situated immediately south of t[
platform end. The tall South Box, whi[
controlled the crossing, is on the right, whilst [
the left is the large water tower. Many engin[
took water at the Junction, and a plentif[
supply was essential.

EVERCREECH JUNCTION

For many years, in the spring and summer, there used to
be a bowl of flowers on the table in the waiting room at
Evercreech Junction. Only a little thing perhaps, but it
was typical of the way in which the Somerset & Dorset
staff always tried to make the travelling public feel
welcome on their line.

155

Evercreech Junction station, looking nor[
from the footbridge on 26th September, 195[
Class 2P, no.40601 has just arrived from Bat[
with the 3.20 p.m. down local. In the midd[
road, the 5.0 p.m. branch local is waiting f[
the 4.15 p.m. Templecombe - Bath to arri[
and then depart north, after which t[
branch-line train will draw forward and the[
set back into the up platform. When the Bat[
Extension was built, the original Somers[
Central Station at Evercreech Junction — as [
then became — was considerably enlarged. Th[
new buildings on the down platform followe[
the same, pleasing style used for other statio[
on the extension, whilst the old Somers[
Central building was added to and converte[
into the station-master's house.

157 The allocation of class 9F, no.92220 *Evening Star* to Bath Motive Power Depot in 1962 to work the "Pines Express" and other heavy trains, had been widely acclaimed. But somehow it seemed rather sad when she appeared again on the Somerset & Dorset in the following summer of 1963, for in the meantime all through traffic had been diverted away from the Somerset & Dorset, and the line had been reduced to a purely local service, run with trains of three or four coaches. So with these, *Evening Star* ambled between Bath and Bournemouth — as she was doing on 12th September, when this picture was taken of her setting off from the Junction with the 1.10 p.m. down local.

156 On a very wet day in May, 1951, ex Midland 0-4-4T, no.58047 — the last Johnson tank on the Somerset & Dorset to retain a round topped firebox and Salter valves on the dome — takes water after arriving with a local off the branch.

158

The down "Pines Express", drawn
S.R. Pacific, no.34040 *Crewkerne* a
B.R. class 5, no.73051, running eas
towards Wyke Champflower on 20
June, 1959, and with speed alrea
being allowed to fall away for t
curves just south of the village.

WYKE CHAMPFLOWER

From Evercreech Junction the Somerset & Dorset
headed south, and as the Mendip hills receded into the
distance, the countryside through which the line was
passing, began to flatten out. In the first 26 miles from
Bath there had been only two level crossings — the
notorious one at Radstock and the second, just south of
Evercreech Junction Station — but now there were two
more within half a mile of each other, both over minor
roads, the second one leading to the village of Wyke
Champflower. As the Somerset & Dorset threaded the
trees on the western edge of this pretty little village, the
line suddenly swung briefly to the east through a sharp
curve, which effectively prevented any fast running in
this vicinity.

159

Ivatt class 2, 2-6-2T, no.41304 heading north from the
Wyke Champflower curves with an afternoon local from
Templecombe to Highbridge in August, 1958.

lass 3F, 0-6-0, no.43218, in charge of ae 2.20 p.m. local from Highbridge Templecombe, passing over the reat Western main line to the West f England on 8th June, 1957. o.43218 — originally S & D J.R., o.73 — was built for the Somerset & orset in 1902 by Neilson, Reid & Co.

APPROACHING COLE

Cole station lay less than a mile south of Wyke Champflower, but before reaching it the Somerset & Dorset had first to cross over the Great Western main line to the West of England via Westbury and Castle Cary, and then Cole viaduct, an elegant structure of five arches, 32´ high.

161 The 3.40 p.m. up from Bournemouth, hauled by B.R. Standard class 4, 2-6-4T, no.80059, crossing over Cole viaduct in the early evening of 26th June, 1965.

COLE

Although only a small village, Cole is of considerable historical railway interest, for it was just north of here, in 1862, that the Somerset Central Railway, extending south east from Glastonbury, met the Dorset Central Railway coming north from Templecombe. The two companies had already arranged to work their lines as one system, and in the same year — 1862 — they were amalgamated to form the Somerset & Dorset Railway.

162 The station at Cole was built by the Dorset Central Railway, and differed in style from those on the Somerset Central Railway. The main building was of typical Dorset Central design with high gables and tall chimneys. No canopy was provided over the platform. On 16th July, 1955 B.R. class 5, no.73073 was passing through the station with the 9.40 a.m. (SO) Sheffield to Bournemouth.

163 The small signal box at Cole was built in the L & S.W.R. style. Approaching on 28th July, 1962 is S & D class 7F, no.53807, returning to Bath, light engine, after working a relief train down to Bournemouth earlier in the day.

164 Class 3F, 0-6-0, no.43218 — old S & D J.R. no.73 — running in with the 2.20 p.m. local from Highbridge to Templecombe on 15th June, 1957. The up starting signal on the left was an interesting adaption of an L & S.W.R. design.

165 The 6.25 a.m. (SO) Cleethorpes to Bournemouth passing through Cole at speed on 14th August, 1954, drawn by class 4F, 0-6-0, no.44102 and S.R. Pacific no.34042 *Dorchester*. The small goods yard on the down side, south of the station, can just be discerned behind the exhaust from the locomotives.

SHEPTON MONTAGUE

The Somerset & Dorset was now passing through some very lovely and unspoilt country. The small villages of Pitcombe and Shepton Montague slipped by on the west side of the line, whilst to the east could be seen Redlynch House, a great mansion set in superb surroundings on the wooded hillside.

166 B.R. class 4, 4-6-0, no.75027 and S.R. Pacific, no.34043 *Combe Martin* running south from Pitcombe towards Shepton Montague with the 10.38 a.m. (SO) Manchester to Bournemouth on 7th July, 1962 — a glorious day with hardly a cloud in the sky.

167 7th July again. The down "Pines Express" passes by, drawn by rebuilt S.R. Pacific, no.34042 *Dorchester*. It is interesting to compare this engine with her unrebuilt sister above.

168 The 4.21 p.m. down semi-fast from Bath, drawn by B.R. 2-6-4T, no.80134, heading south from under a bridge carrying a minor road over the line near Shepton Montague. By Somerset & Dorset standards, the clearance on this bridge was exceptional — 21′2″ from rail level to soffit of arch.

169

S & D class 7F, 2-8-0, no.53810 — one of the 1925 series, rebuilt with a smaller boiler — heading north on 1st September, 1962, in charge of the 10.40 a.m. (SO) Exmouth to Cleethorpes.

NORTH OF WINCANTON

The running now was altogether easier than that encountered north of Evercreech Junction. Adverse gradients were comparatively mild and of no great length, and from Shepton Montague southwards, the line ran absolutely straight for almost two miles — something unheard of between Bath and Evercreech Junction where, if the Somerset & Dorset ran in a straight line for more than half a mile, it was thought remarkable! At the approach to Wincanton the line curved a little to the east before turning due south to pass through the station, built in the usual Dorset Central style, and situated on the western outskirts of the town.

170 After a scheduled two minute stop at Wincanton, B.R. class 4, 4-6-0 no.75072 gathers speed again as she heads north with the 3.40 p.m. up from Bournemouth.

171

Ex G.W.R. 0-6-0, no.3210, with the 4.00 p.m. down local from Highbridge to Templecombe, coming round the curve at the end of the two mile straight from Shepton Montague on 4th August, 1962. The driver had just closed the regulator in preparation for the stop at Wincanton station, half a mile ahead.

172 The down "Pines Express", hauled by rebuilt S.R. Pacific, no.34046 *Braunton*, approaching Horsington on a very hot day in August, 1962.

HORSINGTON

From Wincanton the Somerset & Dorset ran due south for three miles through open country towards the village of Horsington, half a mile north of Templecombe. Just to the south of Horsington Crossing was Templecombe no.3 Junction where a single line — which soon became double — diverged on the down side and then ran parallel with, but at a lower level than, the main line which was climbing on an embankment at 1 in 100. This second line, which was running on the alignment of the original Dorset Central main line, led to the lower yard and the motive power depot. No.3 Junction used to have its own signal box, but in 1933 this was dispensed with, and the points and signals were then power-controlled from no.2 Junction Box.

TEMPLECOMBE

Although little more than a village, Templecombe used to be of considerable railway importance, for as the Somerset & Dorset approached from the north so the Southern main line from Waterloo to the West of England came in from the east. The two lines, both running on embankments, intersected at right angles but just before they met, the Somerset & Dorset dropped down sharply to pass underneath the Southern line.

The two railways were connected by a spur which left the Somerset & Dorset main line at no.2 Junction and continued along an embankment straight towards the Southern line before curving very sharply west to run into a bay platform on the up side of the Southern station.

From no.2 Junction, the Somerset & Dorset main line — now single — dropped down sharply to pass underneath a minor road and then the Southern line. In between these two bridges was "Templecombe Lower", a platform situated on the up side but very little used, since nearly all trains calling at Templecombe, ran into the bay platform at the Southern station — "Templecombe Upper".

The procedure for Somerset & Dorset trains which called at the Southern station was most intriguing. Down trains left the main line at no.2 Junction and ran straight up the spur and into the bay platform. When it was time to set off again, another engine was attached at the rear of the train which was then pulled backwards — with the train engine still coupled on at the other end — to a point north of no.2 Junction. The engine which had drawn the train backwards out of the station was then uncoupled and the train set off again on its journey southwards, bearing left at no.2 Junction and dropping down under the Southern line.

Up trains scheduled to call at Templecombe, came to a stand beyond no.2 Junction. Another engine was then coupled to the rear of the train and drew it backwards up the spur into the station — the train engine remaining attached at the front end throughout the process. When it was time to depart, the train set off down the spur, joining the S & D main line at no.2 Junction and continuing non-stop on its way, the engine which had drawn the train backwards into the station, having been left behind in the platform.

175 No.2 Junction on 31st July, 1954. The train on the left is the 8.48 a.m. up local from Bournemouth. S & D class 7F, no.53800 has just backed on and coupled up and is starting to draw the train backwards up the spur into Templecombe Upper. Standing on the right is S.R. Pacific, no.34040 *Crewkerne*, which had arrived early with the 8.20 a.m. (SO) Bristol to Bournemouth. No.34040 had to wait for the 9.25 a.m. (SO) Bournemouth - Manchester to arrive off the single-line, before she could resume her journey southwards.

31st July, 1954, S & D class 7F, no.53806 — one of 1925 large-boilered series — sweeps up towards no.2 ction with the 10.35 a.m. (SO) Bournemouth to nchester. On the right, class 2P, no.40601 has been d after coming out from the station with the 12.2 p.m. nplecombe - Bath local, and will follow on behind the ress as soon as the line is clear.

G.W.R. 0-6-0, no.3215 pulling out from nplecombe Upper, the 6.5 a.m. Bristol to rnemouth, with the train engine, a B.R. standard s 4, still attached at the other end. Once over the ling points north of no.2 Junction, the train came to tand and the 0-6-0 was detached. The B.R. class 4 n resumed her journey to Bournemouth, setting off n the single-line in the middle foreground.

176 The 7.43 a.m.(SO) Birmingham to Bournemouth, hauled by B.R. class 5, no.73050, had called at Templecombe Upper and then been drawn out backwards to beyond no.2 Junction. Restarting her train for the journey south, no.73050 has just crossed over the trailing points by no.2 Junction Box and is about to collect the tablet prior to bearing left onto the single-line for Stalbridge.

177 Class 9F, 2-10-0, no.92205, sweeping up the sharp rise to no.2 Junction on 13th August, 1960, with the 8.40 a.m. (SO) Bournemouth to Bradford. Templecombe shed can be seen in the distance on the left of this picture.

TEMPLECOMBE

178 Two S & D class 7F-hauled passenger trains on the spur leading from no.2 Junction up to the S.R. station on 16th July, 1955. On the left, no.53804, with the 9.5 a.m. ex Bristol, is in the process of being drawn out backwards from Templecombe Upper so that she can resume her journey to Bournemouth. On the right, no.53807 is running up towards the station with the 7.43 a.m. (SO) Birmingham to Bournemouth.

179
Two generations of tank engines standing outside Templecombe shed in 1955. Ex Midland Johnson 0-4-4T, no.58086, one of a batch introduced in 1881, and ex L.M.S. Ivatt 2-6-2T, no.41249 of 1946.

180
S & D class 7F, no.53802 and two class 3F, 0-6-0s standing on the turntable road. The 50´ turntable, one of the "Balance" type, was just too small to be used by the class 7F, 2-8-0s — a fact which must have been regretted by 7F footplate crews on wet days, when they had to start their return journey to Bath, tender first! (A stop would be made at Evercreech Junction to turn their engine on the table by the North Box.)

181
On 16th July, 1955, ex-Southern class G6, 0-6-0T, no.30274, being used on station pilot duties, was the only S.R. engine on Templecombe shed and, surrounded by L.M. Region types, must have felt "the odd man out"! No.30274 was in the process of being coaled by means of the hoist and tubs seen on the right of the picture.

HENSTRIDGE

From Templecombe no.2 Junction, the Somerset & Dorset became single-line for the next 16 miles as far as Blandford Forum. Henstridge, the first station south of Templecombe, was not a block post and had no passing loop, but there was siding accommodation in a small yard controlled by a ground frame. The single platform was on the up side.

182 Class 9F, 2-10-0, no.92220 *Evening Star*, running south on the single-line from Templecombe towards Henstridge, in charge of the 9.3 a.m. Bristol to Bournemouth.

183 Class 9F, 2-10-0, no.92214, with the 3.40 p.m. up from Bournemouth, standing in Henstridge station where she was booked to stop for one minute.

STALBRIDGE

The first block post south of Templecombe was at Stalbridge. A crossing loop was laid through the station, with the up line being given the straight run through — a principle the Somerset & Dorset followed at all other crossing places on the single-line section between Templecombe and Blandford Forum. The station buildings, on the up side, were of typical Dorset Central design; there was no canopy over the platform. The goods yard was north of the station on the up side. A solid, brick-built signal box controlled a level crossing immediately south of the station.

184 Class 9F, no.92214 running in to Stalbridge with the 3.40 p.m. up from Bournemouth, and crossing the 4.17 p.m. down from Evercreech Junction, hauled by B.R. class 5, no.73051. The 9F has just given up the single-line tablet for the Sturminster Newton - Stalbridge section and has picked up the one for the next section ahead — Stalbridge to no.2 Junction, Templecombe. Stalbridge's red-brick signal box is on the right hand side of the picture.

185 Shortly after passing Henstridge, B.R. class 4, 2-6-0, no.76009 had crossed the county boundary, and was now running through the Dorset countryside south of Stalbridge, in charge of the 4.42 p.m. Templecombe to Bournemouth.

186 On a hot, sultry day in the summer of 1961, class 9F, 2-10-0, no.92001, in charge of the 7.35 a.m. (SO) Nottingham to Bournemouth, rumbles across the lattice-girder bridge over the river Stour north of Sturminster Newton.

187 The 9.3 a.m. Bristol to Bournemouth, hauled by B.R. class 4, 4-6-0, no.75073, running through the deep cutting which led into the station at Sturminster Newton.

STURMINSTER NEWTON

Four miles running south east from Stalbridge, brought the Somerset & Dorset to Sturminster Newton, a small market town delightfully situated on the peaceful, meandering river Stour. Approaching from the north west, the line crossed over the Stour on a lattice-girder bridge and then passed through a short, deep cutting, to run into the station. As at Stalbridge, the buildings followed the standard Dorset Central style although, rather unusually, the platforms were slightly staggered. The spacious goods yard, on the east side of the station, had a red-brick goods shed and ample facilities for loading cattle — as befitted a busy market town. The signal box at Sturminster Newton was built of wood in the L & S.W.R. style, and stood at the southern end of the up platform.

188 On 22nd August, 1959, S & D class 7F, 2-8-0, no.53804 — returning light-engine to Bath, tender first, after working a special down to Poole earlier in the day — was standing by Sturminster Newton signal box, waiting for the single-line section to Stalbridge. After about five minutes, S & D class 4F, 0-6-0, no.44561 ran in with the 12.23 p.m. down local from Templecombe to Bournemouth, and the signalman can be seen on his way over to the engine to exchange tablets. Shortly afterwards, the class 7F was able to resume her long — and no doubt, rather tedious — journey home.

189

A bird's eye view of Sturminster Newton station, looking south, showing how the up road had the straight run through the loop. Standing in the station on a misty day in early autumn 1963, is B.R. class 5, no.73052 with the 3.40 p.m. up from Bournemouth.

STURMINSTER NEWTON

191 "Big pouch" exchange. B.R. 2-6-2T, no.82039, heading north with the 4.45 p.m. Bailey Gate - Templecombe milk train, was not fitted with a mechanical catcher, so the fireman and signalman exchanged tablets by hand, using "Big pouches".

190 B.R. class 4, 2-6-0, no.76061, running in with the 1.10 p.m. up local from Bournemouth on 2nd September, 1961, crosses class 9F, 2-10-0, no.92000 in charge of the 7.35 a.m. (SO) Nottingham to Bournemouth.

SHILLINGSTONE

After three miles running south east from Sturminster Newton, in the course of which the line passed over the Stour again, the Somerset & Dorset arrived at Shillingstone. The station, located on the northern edge of the village, was a rather more refined version of the Dorset Central design. The buildings were on the up platform, which had the unusual feature of being provided with an ornate canopy. The small L & S.W.R. style signal box stood on the up side at the northern end of the station, beyond which was the goods yard.

192 The large, Southern Region "Merchant Navy" Pacifics were prohibited from running over the Somerset & Dorset because of their weight. But by January, 1966, with the closure of the line only weeks away, nothing really mattered any more, so no objections were raised when S.R. Pacific no.35011 *General Steam Navigation*, was used to haul one of the many farewell excursions being run over the Somerset & Dorset. On 1st January, 1966, no.35011, in charge of a special organised by the Locomotive Club of Great Britain, was heading north from the station, past the goods yard from which the track had already been lifted.

3 L.M.S. Ivatt 2-6-2T, no.41243 nning in to Shillingstone station th the 3.35 p.m. down local from mplecombe to Blandford Forum. he return working was the 4.45 p.m. iley Gate - Templecombe milk in.)

194 Class 9F, 2-10-0, no.92006 nearing Blandford Forum on 19th August, 1961, with the 7.35 a.m. (SO) Nottingham to Bournemouth.

SHILLINGSTONE TO BLANDFORD FORUM

Two miles south of Shillingstone, the Somerset & Dorset again crossed over the Stour, and then as the hills began to close in from the east, the line commenced climbing at 1 in 80, turning through a long, sweeping curve towards the south. The approach to Blandford Forum was through a lengthy cutting, with the line descending at 1 in 80 over the last ¾ mile before arriving at the station, conveniently set near the centre of the town.

195 The 12.10 p.m. (SO) Bournemouth to Nottingham, drawn by rebuilt S.R. Pacific, no.34039 *Boscastle*, running north up the Stour valley towards Shillingstone on a hazy day in July, 1961.

BLANDFORD FORUM

t Blandford Forum, the single-line section from emplecomble came to an end, the Somerset & Dorset everting to double track for the next eight miles as far as orfe Mullen. The station at Blandford Forum was an nlarged version of the standard Dorset Central design. he main buildings were, as usual, on the up platform hich was adorned with a rather cumbersome canopy, hilst a small building on the down platform was ominated by the tall signal box. The well laid out goods ard was situated on the east side of the station. mmediately south of Blandford Forum, the Somerset & orset crossed the Stour for the last time.

196 The 9.40 a.m. up local from Bournemouth, hauled by S.R. Pacific no.34041 *Wilton*, standing in Blandford Forum station on 30th March, 1964.

197

S.R. Pacific, no.34103 *Calstock* makes a brisk start from Blandford Forum with an up train for Bath. Ahead lies the single-line to Shillingstone, rising at 1 in 80 for the first ¾ mile.

198 S & D class 7F, 2-8-0, no.53804, with the 9.8 a.m. (SO) Birmingham to Bournemouth, dips down a short length of 1 in 100 to pass under the road bridge just north of Charlton Marshall Halt.

CHARLTON MARSHALL

Two miles south of Blandford Forum, the Somerset & Dorset passed by the village of Charlton Marshall. When this section of the Dorset Central had been opened in 1860, the villagers of Charlton Marshall were disappointed that no station had been provided for them. Some 68 years later — in 1928 — this omission was corrected when a small halt was built just south of a road overbridge to the west of Charlton Marshall. But alas the inhabitants of Charlton Marshall did not have long to enjoy their new facility, for the halt was closed in 1956 — anticipating, by ten years, the end of the Somerset & Dorset.

199 The 1.10 p.m. up local from Bournemouth, hauled by B.R. class 4, 2-6-0, no.76064, comes up through the trees towards the halt on 3rd September, 1960.

200 Some of the fastest running on the Somerset & Dorset was done between Blandford Forum and Corfe Mullen. On 19th August, 1961, rebuilt S.R. Pacific, no.34039 *Boscastle*, was approaching Spetisbury close on 70 m.p.h. with the 12.20 p.m. (SO) Bournemouth to Nottingham.

BETWEEN SPETISBURY AND BAILEY GATE

From Blandford Forum southwards, through Spetisbury and Bailey Gate to Corfe Mullen, was some of the easiest running on the whole of the Somerset & Dorset. Over this eight miles of double track there were no gradients of any consequence, no curves of any severity, and no speed-restricting passing loops with which to contend.

201 On a lovely day in late summer, 1960, B.R. class 4, 4-6-0, no.75027 was running north from Bailey Gate through the rolling, open countryside with the 11.12 a.m. (SO) Bournemouth to Sheffield.

202 S & D class 7F, 2-8-0, no.53802 heading north from Corfe Mullen signal box with the 12.55 p.m. up local from Bournemouth on 9th July, 1955.

CORFE MULLEN

When the Dorset Central Railway was built, the line ran east from Corfe Mullen to join the London & South Western Railway by a trailing junction at Wimborne. This meant that all down Somerset & Dorset trains had to reverse at Wimborne before they could set off over the L & S.W.R. line for Bournemouth. A similar process, of course, had to be gone through by up S & D trains from Bournemouth to the North. In 1884/5 the Somerset & Dorset built a new line, three miles long, from Corfe Mullen to join the London & South Western Railway at Broadstone. This not only shortened the distance between Bath and Bournemouth, but also saved considerable time by cutting out the tedious reversal procedure previously necessary for all S & D trains at Wimborne.

203

On 14th August, 1954, the 9.18 a.m. (SO) Birmingham to Bournemouth, hauled by two B.R. class 5s, nos.73052 and 73050, joined the single-line at Corfe Mullen for the three mile run to Broadstone. The other track in this picture was the original Dorset Central line to Wimborne. The eastern end of this had been lifted in 1933, but a mile of track remained at the Corfe Mullen end to serve Carter's siding. The two class 5s hauling this train were only a few months old. Together with sister engine no.73051 they had been allocated to Bath Motive Power Depot early in May 1954, when brand-new.

204 On a miserable day in August, 1954, S & D class 7F 2-8-0 no.53810, in charge of a relief from Leicester, threads the sand cutting above Broadstone in a blustering south west wind.

NEARING BROADSTONE

At Corfe Mullen the Somerset & Dorset became single-line again for the comparatively short run to Broadstone. Although this section was only three miles long, it included a formidable bank, the line climbing at 1 in 80 for nearly 1½ miles. The summit came in a sand cutting bordered with clusters of pine trees and patches of heather and gorse — a delightful spot on a warm summer's day. After a brief level stretch, the line started to descend at 1 in 97, bisecting a golf course and dropping smoothly straight down into Broadstone.

205 Class 4F 0-6-0, no.44417 breasts the summit of the climb from Corfe Mullen, with the 12.23 p.m. down local from Templecombe, on 3rd October, 1959.

BROADSTONE

With the ending at Broadstone of the three mile single-line section from Corfe Mullen, also ended the Somerset & Dorset's own track, for at Broadstone, connection was made with the old London & South Western Railway, and S & D trains used the Southern line for the last eight miles of their journey to Bournemouth.

206 S.R. Pacific, no.34043 *Combe Martin*, in charge of the 9.40 a.m. (SO) Sheffield to Bournemouth, coasts down off the S & D single-line from Corfe Mullen, to join the Southern line at Broadstone.

207 After reaching the top of Broadstone bank and passing through the station, B.R. class 5, no.73087 swings north onto the S & D single-line for Corfe Mullen with the 10.5 a.m. (SO) Bournemouth to Derby. In the immediate foreground is the line from Brockenhurst and Wimborne. The line passing straight through the station went to Hamworthy Junction.

BROADSTONE BANK

From Broadstone, the line to Bournemouth immediately started to descend at 1 in 75, and was soon well below the level of the line to Hamworthy Junction, with which it had set off from Broadstone side by side. After dropping downhill for two miles, the railway was almost down to sea level and drawing near to Holes Bay — and the smell of the sea was already in the air.

208
1 in 75 up, and twelve on! S.R. Pacific no.34102 *Lapford* was coming up Broadstone bank in a very determined style on 16th July, 1960, with the 9.25 a.m. (SO) Bournemouth to Liverpool.

HOLES BAY JUNCTION

As Somerset & Dorset trains drew near to Poole, the Southern main line from Weymouth to Waterloo could be seen skirting round Holes Bay on a low embankment, and soon this came trailing in to join the line from Broadstone at Holes Bay Junction, half a mile north of Poole.

209
S & D class 7F, 2-8-0, no.53808 passing Holes Bay Junction as she runs towards Poole with the 7.43 a.m. (SO) Birmingham to Bournemouth. Coming in from the left is the Southern main line from Weymouth to Waterloo.

PARKSTONE BANK

At Poole, all trains had to make a compulsory stop. On leaving the station, the line curved sharply south east, passing over two very busy level-crossings in the town, and then, with the waters of Parkstone Bay bordering the line to the south, came Parkstone bank — 1¼ miles of very tough climbing at 1 in 60 up to Branksome.

211
Halfway up Parkstone bank, the gradient eased briefly to 1 in 300 through Parkstone station, only for the 1 in 60 to set in again immediately after the platform end. Class 9F, 2-10-0, no.92214 has just passed through the station and is tackling the second part of the 1 in 60 in great style with the 9.3 a.m. Bristol to Bournemouth (9.55 a.m. ex Bath).

210 S.R. Pacific, no.34041 *Wilton* with a Southern Region train of empty stock skirts Parkstone Bay at the start of the 1 in 60 climb up Parkstone bank on 3rd October, 1959.

212 B.R. class 5, no.73092 had steam to spare as she neared the end of the second stretch of 1 in 60 with the 8.50 a.m. excursion from Bristol on August Bank Holiday Monday 1964. (Note the ex L.N.E.R. articulated stock next to the engine.)

213 On 3rd August, 1964, ex L.M.S. class 8F, 2-8-0, no.48470 was descending the bank with the 1.10 p.m. local from Bournemouth to Bath.

BOURNEMOUTH WEST

After reaching the top of Parkstone bank, the line passed through Branksome station, and then came Branksome Junction where the London line — which ran through Bournemouth Central station — diverged to the left. Somerset & Dorset trains took the right hand fork and after passing the small S & D engine shed set within the Branksome triangle, and then the carriage sidings and washing plant, dropped down the final ¼ mile at 1 in 90 into the terminus, Bournemouth West. The 71½-mile journey from Bath was over.

214 On 14th August, 1954, the 6.55 a.m. down local from Bath arrived at Bournemouth West hauled by S & D class 7F, 2-8-0, no.53805 — one of the 1914 series.

215 A little later in the morning, sister engine, no.53806 — one of the 1925 large-boilered engines — was preparing to leave with the 12.25 p.m. (SO) to Birmingham.

216 S & D class 4F, 0-6-0, no.44561 setting off from Bournemouth West with the 3.35 p.m. to Bristol on 10th August, 1954. As this train, carrying mail, made a connection at Mangotsfield with the evening mail train from Bristol to the North, nothing was allowed to delay her run up the S & D to Bath, and she was given priority over all other trains on the single-line sections.

217 Ten years later, the same train — then timed to leave 5 minutes later at 3.40 p.m. — set off behind class 9F, 2-10-0, no.92214.

THE BRANCH

The single-line running west for 24 miles from Evercreech Junction over to Burnham-on-Sea, was originally part of the main line of the Somerset & Dorset, until superseded in 1874 by the "Bath Extension" — the new line from Evercreech Junction to Bath — when it became "The Branch".

The characteristics of "The Branch" were the complete opposite to those of the "Bath Extension". Whereas the line from Evercreech Junction to Bath abounded in curves and long, fearsome gradients, "The Branch" — after descending Pylle bank — ran dead straight, and virtually level, for mile after mile. A feature of the branch was the number of level-crossings over minor by-ways, each with its attendant crossing-keeper's house. Because of their remote situation, many of these crossing-keeper's houses had no water supply and so this was delivered by the morning up goods train in five gallon milk churns — carried on the engine! The turn was often referred to as "The tea run" — because of the number of cups of tea offered to the train crew by crossing keepers' wives when the water was delivered.

PYLLE

The branch left the main line at Evercreech Junction North and curving gently towards the west, arrived, after two miles, at Pylle. The station situated immediately to the west of the Shepton Mallet - Ilchester road, was over a mile from the village, which was rather hard luck on the villagers, the more so since, after leaving the station, the line passed within a ¼ mile of the village. From Pylle the line descended on a ruling gradient of 1 in 88, dropping down through Pylle woods and heading towards West Pennard.

218   For many years the Branch was the happy domain of Johnson's class 3F, 0-6-0 tender engines and 0-4-4 tank engines. On 14th April, 1955, class 3F, no.43218 — built for the S & D.J.R. in 1902 by Neilson, Reid & Co. — was setting off from Pylle with the 5.0 p.m. local from Evercreech Junction to Highbridge.

219

Class 3F, 0-6-0, no.43356 — an ex-Midland engine — dropping downhill through Pylle woods on 21st May, 1956, with an excursion from Templecombe to Burnham-on-Sea.

WEST PENNARD

3½ miles west of Pylle was West Pennard station, the first block post and crossing place since the branch left Evercreech Junction. (Pylle ceased to be a block post in 1929 when the crossing-loop was removed.) The station buildings and signal box were on the up side. As at Pylle, the inhabitants of West Pennard had a long walk to reach their station which was situated on the Shepton Mallet - Glastonbury road, some two miles from the village. The branch now ran dead straight for the next four miles towards Glastonbury.

220 Ex G.W.R. 0-6-0, no.3206 leaving West Pennard on 3rd November, 1962, with the 2.20 p.m. down local from Highbridge. The line, which ran dead straight for four miles, can be seen disappearing into the distance.

221

Another ex G.W.R. 0-6-0, no.3215, passes the attractive West Pennard up starting signal, as she runs in with a pick-up goods from Highbridge to Evercreech Junction on a misty morning in October, 1962.

GLASTONBURY

Glastonbury had one of the most attractive stations on the Somerset & Dorset. There were wooden buildings on both the up and down platforms which had ornate umbrella-style awnings, and were joined by a covered footbridge over the lines. The down platform also had an outer face, which was used by trains that ran over the 5½ mile branch to Wells until this was closed in 1951. An imposing signal box stood at the west end of the up platform, beyond which was a goods yard of considerable size.

222 The S & D class 7F 2-8-0s did not often run over the branch, where they were limited — officially — to 30 m.p.h. However, on 7th June, 1964, no.53807 assisted S & D class 4F 0-6-0, no.44558 with an enthusiasts excursion, seen here nearing Glastonbury at the end of the four mile straight run from West Pennard.

223

The 2.20 p.m. down local from Highbridge setting off from Glastonbury in October, 1964, hauled by G.W.R. 0-6-0, no.2217.

NEAR CATCOTT

Over the next twelve miles, between Glastonbury and Highbridge, there were four small stations — at Ashcott, Shapwick, Edington Junction and Bason Bridge. Of these, only Shapwick and Edington Junction were block posts. Around Shapwick the line passed between vast fields of peat, which produced considerable traffic for Shapwick station. Edington Junction was where the Bridgwater branch swung away south west. After this branch was closed in 1954, the station was renamed Edington Burtle. At Bason Bridge there is a large milk factory, and thousands of gallons of milk used to be dispatched daily by rail.

As the branch ran westwards, the countryside through which the line was passing was one of flat meadows and numerous water-courses — lush and beautiful in summer, but waterlogged and desolate in winter.

224 One of several farewell excursions run over the Somerset & Dorset on the last week-end of the line's existence. Two Ivatt 2-6-2Ts, nos. 41307 and 41269, nearing Catcott on Saturday, 5th March, 1966, in charge of a special train organised by the Locomotive Club of Great Britain.

225 On a calm day in early spring 1965, S & D class 4F, 0-6-0, no.44560 and her excursion train were mirrored in the still water beside the line as they headed east from Edington Burtle.

HIGHBRIDGE

As the line approached Highbridge, the Motive Power Depot and the old Somerset & Dorset Locomotive, Carriage & Wagon Works — closed in 1930 — were passed on the south side. On the down side stood a signal box — the first of four at Highbridge — beyond which was the station, with two through platforms and three terminal ones, and situated right alongside the G.W.R. station. Immediately west of the station, the S & D crossed the G.W.R. on the level. All movements over this intersection were controlled by the G.W.R. signal box, although until the First World War, the S & D had a small box, Highbridge A, at the end of platform 4, which worked in conjunction with the G.W.R. box. To the west of the crossing came another small box, Highbridge B, which controlled movements into the goods yard, and then 300 yards further west, there was yet another little box, Highbridge C, controlling the entrance to the wharf sidings and also the level crossing gates over a busy main road.

226 A down local from Burnham-on-Sea, hauled by class 3F, 0-6-0, no.43194 — built for the S & D at Derby in 1896 — heading east past Highbridge B box and about to cross the G.W.R. main line on the level.

227 Ex G.W.R. 0-6-0, no.3206 waiting to leave Highbridge in July 1963, with the 2.20 p.m. down local. On the left of the picture can be seen the old S & D, "A" box, disused as a signal box since 1914.

BURNHAM-ON-SEA

1¾ miles west of Highbridge, the Branch finally came to an end at Burnham-on-Sea, 24 miles from Evercreech Junction. The small terminus had an all-over roof and one short platform, on the eastern end of which stood a little signal cabin. A longer platform on the south side of the original station had been added later to accommodate lengthy excursion trains. Regular passenger services between Highbridge and Burnham-on-Sea ceased in October, 1951, but excursion trains continued to work through to the terminus until September, 1962.

228 S & D class 3F, 0-6-0, no.43194 standing in Burnham-on-Sea station with a down local. Note the little signal cabin on the end of the platform.

29

o mark the centenary of the opening of the merset Central Railway between Glastonry and Highbridge on 28th August, 1854, a ecial train was run from Glastonbury to rnham-on-Sea and back on 28th August, 54. (The reason for continuing on from ghbridge to Burnham-on-Sea was rather scure, as this section was not opened until 58.) The engine chosen to haul the train was ss 3F, 0-6-0 no.43201, built for the S & D at rby in 1896. For the event the class 3F rried her original number, 64, and the letters D.J.R. on her buffer beam and tender sides. the picture, the train is seen about to set off m Burnham-on-Sea on the return run to astonbury.

THE BRIDGWATER BRANCH

A branch left the Evercreech Junction-Burnham-on-Sea line at Edington Junction and ran 7 miles south west to Bridgwater. There was one intermediate station at Cossington and a halt at Bawdrip; neither was a block post. The Bridgwater branch was opened in 1890, and closed in 1954.

230

0-4-4T, no.58073 running west from Bawdrip with the 3.30 p.m. goods from Edington Junction to Bridgwater in August, 1953.

HIGHBRIDGE MOTIVE POWER DEPOT

The Motive Power Depot at Highbridge was situated on the south side of the line, next to the old Somerset & Dorset Locomotive, Carriage & Wagon Works — closed in 1930. The engine shed had two roads and there was a 49′9″ turn-table.

231 For many years, the Johnson 0-4-4 tanks and class 3F, 0-6-0 tender engines had been the backbone of the motive power on the Branch. Four of the 0-4-4Ts are seen here, lined up outside the shed one Sunday morning in August, 1953. The engines are nos.58086, 58073, 58051 and 58072.

232 When the Johnson tanks at last started to feel their age, the type that began to replace them was Ivatt's 2-6-2T design of 1946. On 12th August, 1951, Ivatt 2-6-2T, no.41241 was standing beside Johnson 0-4-4T, no.58047 — the last of these engines on the S & D to retain a round topped firebox and Salter valves on the dome.

No.58047 was broken-up many years ago, but happily no.41241 has survived and is now running, in immaculate condition, on the Keighley & Worth Valley Railway.

233 Two class 3F, 0-6-0s standing beside the water tower in the summer of 1953. No.43419 was an ex Midland engine, whilst no.43218 was built for the Somerset & Dorset in 1902 by Neilson, Reid & Co.

234

Two of the Johnson 0-4-4Ts, nos.58073 and 58051, standing outside the two-road engine shed.

235 The end came for the Somerset & Dorset on Sunday, 6th March, 1966. As dusk began to fall, the last of the special trains had gone, and Midford's down home signal, standing gaunt against the evening sky, would not be lowered again.

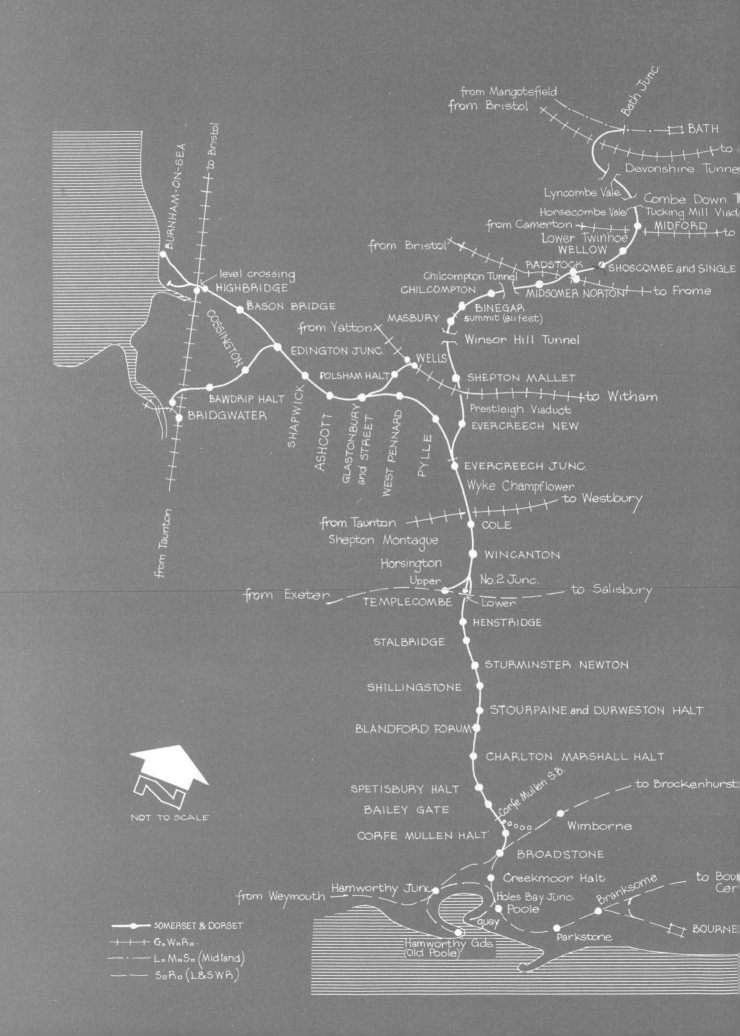

BURNHAM-ON-SEA

to Bristol

level crossing
HIGHBRIDGE

BASON BRIDGE

COSSINGTON

BAWDRIP HALT

BRIDGWATER

SHAPWICK

from Taunton

ASHCOTT

GLASTONBURY and STREET

WEST PENNARD

EDINGTON JUNC.

POLSHAM HALT

from Yatton

WELLS

PYLLE

from Mangotsfield
from Bristol

Bath Junc.

BATH

to

Devonshire Tunnel

Lyncombe Vale

Horsecombe Vale

from Camerton

Lower Twinhoe

Combe Down T

Tucking Mill Viad.

MIDFORD

to

WELLOW

RADSTOCK

SHOSCOMBE and SINGLE

Chilcompton Tunnel

CHILCOMPTON

MASBURY

BINEGAR
summit (811 feet)

MIDSOMER NORTON

to Frome

Winsor Hill Tunnel

SHEPTON MALLET

to Witham

Prestleigh Viaduct

EVERCREECH NEW

EVERCREECH JUNC.

Wyke Champflower

to Westbury

from Taunton

Shepton Montague

COLE

Horsington

WINCANTON

Upper

No.2 Junc.

to Salisbury

from Exeter

TEMPLECOMBE

Lower

HENSTRIDGE

STALBRIDGE

STURMINSTER NEWTON

SHILLINGSTONE

STOURPAINE and DURWESTON HALT

BLANDFORD FORUM

CHARLTON MARSHALL HALT

SPETISBURY HALT

Corfe Mullen S.B.

to Brockenhurst

BAILEY GATE

Corfe Mullen

Wimborne

CORFE MULLEN HALT

BROADSTONE

Creekmoor Halt

Branksome

to Bou
Cer

from Weymouth

Hamworthy Junc.

Holes Bay Junc.

Poole

quay

Parkstone

BOURNE

Hamworthy Gds
(Old Poole)

NOT TO SCALE

SOMERSET & DORSET
G.W.R.
L.M.S. (Midland)
S.R. (L&SWR)